Mom,
Happy Birthday
1, September 1995

Love
Pam and Bruce

Mom,
Happy Birthday

The M. I. Hummel Album

The
M. I. Hummel
Album

Galahad Books · New York

Published in 1994 by

Galahad Books
A division of Budget Book Service, Inc.
386 Park Avenue South
New York, NY 10016

Galahad Books is a registered trademark of Budget Book Service, Inc.

Published by arrangement with Portfolio Press.

Library of Congress Catalog Card Number: 91-90525

ISBN: 0-88365-878-X

Printed in the United States of America.

CONTENTS

PHOTOGRAPHY: WALTER PFEIFFER
TEXT (Chapters 2, 3 and 4): JOAN N. OSTROFF
*The publisher acknowledges with gratitude the help of Manfred Arras in
preparing the text.*

All the changes in the world today are happening so fast it's hard to keep up with them. In Germany alone, the changes are dramatic and exciting.

What better talisman for the brightness of the future can there be but M. I. Hummel figurines, those wonderful depictions of love and trust introduced by my father in the mid-1930s. Their brightness continues to shine, and continues to demand attention. So much so that, although the definitive Golden Anniversary Album was published in 1984, the growth of the interest in these ceramic children has pushed beyond the pages of that book and necessitated this updated edition.

At Goebel, too, we have undergone many changes in order to keep up with an evolving world and its developing technologies. But one thing will never change: our family spirit, which is felt by all those involved in the creation of M. I. Hummel figurines, many of whose forebears were part of the Goebel team in our earliest days. Although M. I. Hummel figurines were introduced to the world in 1935, the foundations of Goebel expertise were established in 1871, when the company was founded by my great-great-grandfather and his son.

Today the figurines represent the continuity of life. They remind us of our own childhood, show us the children of today, and help us look to the future. They demonstrate for us the resiliency and strength of humanity. For many people everywhere in the world, they have become a constant source of pleasure and inspiration. It is with a sense of great pride that we acknowledge this.

I dedicate this book to collectors everywhere, whether they have been collectors for years or are just getting started. I hope it will delight you, and that you will feel the brightness shining through.

Wilhelm Goebel

Wilhelm Goebel
Roedental, Bavaria
Federal Republic of Germany

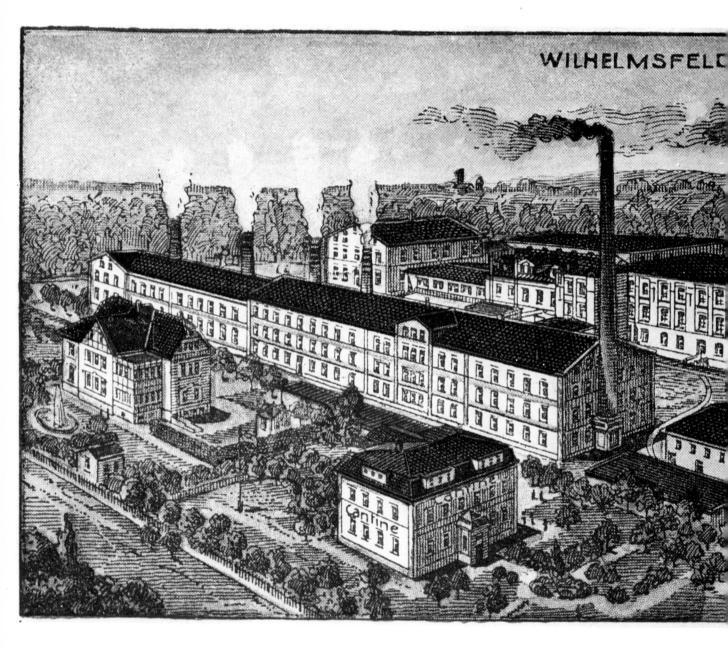

WILHELMSFELD

A Celebration of Life

Since M. I. Hummel figurines first appeared in the 1930s, millions of people the world over have succumbed to their charms. Why are these figurines considered the world's most beloved collectibles? The universal appeal of children is an obvious answer, but this is only a general response. Hummel figurines are indeed *gemuetlich*, that special German word that can be translated as good-natured, cheerful and cozy. But their enduring appeal is the result of a unique collaboration: the original art of Sister Maria Innocentia Hummel and its matchless interpretation by the artisans at W. Goebel Porzellanfabrik, which together create a romantic and stylized sense of childhood in a folkloric, timeless fashion.

Nationality and background are irrelevant to those who collect M. I. Hummel figurines. What does matter is that, with deceptively simple strokes, the artist has captured the very essence of childhood: the innocence, the eagerness to learn and to absorb, the trust with which these small creatures face the world, and the self-assurance with which they hand down to the younger ones the lessons they have already learned.

The figurines are valid representations of the drawn artwork, reiterating their vitality through the addition of the third dimension. Since the early days in the mid-1930s, a key to their appeal continues to be the quality of handcraftsmanship. With caring hands, Goebel artisans treat each piece as something special, something that will eventually charm and delight an unseen collector very far away.

For a better understanding of their ongoing allure let's look into their background more closely. To do this, we'll touch on the history of a company, a country, an industry, and come to understand the deep humanity of those involved.

The Early Years

The porcelain-producing firm of W. Goebel Porzellanfabrik was founded by Franz Detleff Goebel and his son William in 1871 in the town today known as Roedental, in the county of Coburg. Around the turn of the century, figurines were added to the production of tableware at the firm. By the mid-1930s, Goebel had become a name well known in the international marketplace. But that was a period of uncertainty and change.

Times were very bad in Germany; the post-World War I depression lingered. There were four hundred employees at the factory who needed more work. Franz Goebel, the fourth-generation owner of the firm and a member of a family traditionally concerned with social welfare, wanted to be sure he was able to continue to employ his staff and continue the family business. The timing was critical for the development of something new, to put new life into the company's output.

The Search

Franz had a deep-rooted feeling that the ideal new line should represent children. Children generally were shown in porcelain only as cherubs or angels, not in a "natural" form. In literature, they had been celebrated for generations in *Maerchen*, or fairy tales, which were often used by parents to instruct their own children in proper behavior. The legends brought families together around the comforting fire as stories were read aloud. With unrest building in the world, it would be timely, Franz reasoned, to create this image of warmth and understanding. But to do this he needed to find the right artist, one whose sympathies and appreciation of children transcended the commonplace. One who could look into the heart of a child and find—and express—love.

In December 1934, to see how sales were progressing, he, along with Ernst Steiner, a sales representative, visited some of his customers in Munich. At Steiner's suggestion, they included a few religious card shops on their itinerary. There Franz found his artist, for the art cards of Sister Maria Innocentia Hummel were on display. Excited by the idea of turning these images into figurines, he took some cards back with him to Coburg, to discuss with his master sculptors, Reinhold Unger and Arthur Moeller. His enthusiasm was contagious; they, too, responded with excitement.

Franz contacted the artist at the Convent of Siessen, the Franciscan religious order of which she was a member, in hopes of receiving her permission to proceed. Since Sister Maria Innocentia Hummel was not a sculptor, she questioned whether three-dimensional renderings of her two-dimensional art could be proper translations of her work.

So began the quest, to determine if the factory could indeed translate the artist's vision. Creative energy ran high; it was concluded that figurines could be sculpted from the original art, and an entirely new palette of ceramic colors was created to carry out the special feeling inherent in the paintings. A radical change in the production process was made, which has proved to be of great and long-lasting importance. Although the company was known primarily for porcelain, it was determined that the unique character of Sister M. I. Hummel's art would be better served with the warmer feel of fine earthenware, which had been pioneered by Goebel in the mid-1920s.

Franz then assured the artist that she would check the correctness of the three-dimensional interpretation and the colors of each model to be produced. In addition, as a sign of her approval, he guaranteed that a facsimile of her signature would appear on each piece. He also promised her that he himself would take direct charge of quality control, to ensure that only the finest pieces would be produced. Those stipulations clear, the artist agreed by letter on January 9, 1935 and with a license agreement signed, the work began in earnest!

Sister Maria Innocentia Hummel's religious holiday cards gained popularity while she was still a Franciscan candidate at the Siessen Convent.

During 1935 Franz Goebel worked closely with his two master sculptors, Arthur Moeller (top) and Reinhold Unger (above) to develop the first figurines based on Sister Maria Innocentia Hummel's art.

History is Made

Franz and his brother-in-law and partner, Dr. Eugen Stocke, planned the introduction for the Leipzig Trade Fair, the major show for the industry. It brought attendees from across the seas, as well as from all areas of Europe. It was here that American distributors came to see the latest European products. Because Goebel had a tradition of the new and the novel, there was always an incentive to visit its display.

The fair was scheduled for March, just a few weeks away; there was no time to lose. The intoxicating activity reached a new high as all the challenges presented by the innovative concept were met. True to his promise to Sister Maria Innocentia, Franz himself was at the forefront of all phases of production, helping to devise the unprecedented techniques that this new line necessitated. Working around the clock, the sculptors, moldmakers, assemblers, decorators and all the workers at the factory were swept up in the excitement.

And so began the history that continues to enchant. The introduction brought with it interest and acceptance; so much so, that by the end of that year there were forty-six motifs on the market. Because of positive projections by Marshall Field & Co. of Chicago and other American retailers, fifteen more had been added to the line by the end of 1936.

In August of the same year, Sister Maria Innocentia visited the factory. It was a day long remembered as one of great importance.

The Brutal Years

But the world had begun its reckless spin into madness. The rise of Nazism brought with it brutality and cruelty. In early 1937, the Hitler government issued a decree against all private and Church-run schools in a major step to remove religious influence from education. Royalties paid to the Convent by Goebel helped it in those difficult times.

On the international front, a war of global implications was imminent. In 1939, many in the United States began a boycott of German goods, which led to a dramatic decrease in production at Goebel. When World War II began, Goebel adhered to government directives and channeled its production primarily to dinnerware for the armed forces.

With the war's end in 1945, the great deprivation and hardship continued. But now a new threat appeared on the horizon, for Germany was being divided among the allies. Coburg, in Northeast Bavaria near the Czechoslovakian border, ultimately was declared to be in the U.S. Zone, but not before weeks of uncertainty held the region in dreadful suspense.

FORMEREI

Early production was often a painstaking trial-and-error experience. Among the pieces from this early production are many with variations. The process included (clockwise from top left): Filling the old round charcoal heated kiln, 1937; Enamel firing, 1937; Glazing by hand, 1936; Mold making, 1935; Master painter Louis Knauer at work, 1936; Assembling a figurine, 1937.

Sister Maria Innocentia (right) is seen with Franz Goebel during one of his visits to the Convent of Siessen. Sister Laura is at left.

Opposite page:
Sister Maria Innocentia's love for children is quite evident in this drawing.

For many days it was not known where the line would be drawn. Just eight miles away, in Sonneberg. Soviet troops awaited the outcome of negotiations, ready to move in as soon as the order was given. The Coburgers waited in their homes. Finally, the decision was made. The Soviet Zone would begin six miles to the east of Coburg, outside Neustadt, with Coburg left in a pocket surrounded on three sides by East Germany.

Life Begins Again

The work at the factory had ground to a halt, yet employees who had been called to war were returning to the area. Because the U.S. government was interested in reactivating industry, particularly so close to the Communist border of East Germany, Goebel was among those companies given permission to manufacture and export once again. But it was a slow start; many of the molds from before the war were broken or lost, and the modeling of some of the established motifs had to be done all over again. In some cases, changes were made from the original designs (with approval received from Sister Maria Innocentia) to better serve production requirements.

Thanks to helpful aid received from friends of the factory in America, and to the resourcefulness of the Coburgers themselves, production was able to resume despite early shortages of raw materials and food. In 1946, restrictions against fraternization between American G.I.'s and Germans were lifted, and the many friendships that developed were also a helpful source, for the soldiers proved generous with food and other supplies.

In time, the Americans began to see M. I. Hummel figurines in the shops, and became intrigued by the fresh-faced sunny ceramic children. Not only did they begin to buy them; they also found that they could be bartered, for cigarettes, chocolates, and other scarce commodities. Now that the soldiers' families were coming over to join them, the search for the figurines soon became a special activity. In fact, collecting M. I. Hummel figurines was listed as a formal recommendation of the U.S. Army in its guidebook for army personnel.

Soon the figurines began to be shipped to the States as gifts or as part of households relocating back home. Eventually this led to an increase in demand on the U.S. market and retailers reported escalation of sales.

In the midst of all this new-found optimism came the tragic death of the artist herself. Never robust, she had always worked to serve others, even during the years of greatest hardship. She lived under conditions of extreme deprivation, yet continued to cheer others with her sketches designed to uplift the spirit. Sister Maria Innocentia fell victim to a chronic illness and on November 6, 1946, at the hour of noon, she died.

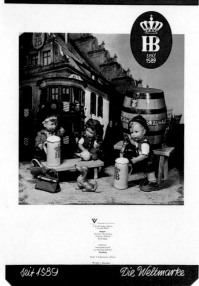

Top:
Like many German products manufactured after World War II, M. I. Hummel figurines were stamped with a U.S. Zone mark to note their origin for export purposes.

Above:
During the late 1960s American tourists were flocking to Germany. What could have been a better combination than the Hofbrauhaus and M. I. Hummel, as featured on this calendar?

But the production of her figurines continued. Ever a prolific artist, she left behind a great legacy of two-dimensional art that continues to this day to provide the inspiration for new figurine motifs. And the process set in motion by Franz Goebel and the Convent of Siessen in 1935, with the signing of the licensing agreement, still exists: that both clay models and decorated figurines are brought to the Convent for approval by an artistic board whose mandate it is to carry out the legacy of M. I. Hummel.

In the summer of 1969 there was another major blow. Plans were underway for a great celebration for Franz Goebel's birthday; sadly, he died unexpectedly just days before the scheduled event. Now his son Wilhelm and nephew Ulrich Stocke, along with his brother-in-law Eugen Stocke, inherited the role of leadership.

Years of Development

The years of a divided Germany continued to be years of development for Goebel and the figurines. American collectors by the thousands visited the factory annually, bringing with them questions about production, about the artist, about the variations in motifs they always seemed to find. By the early 1970s, it became apparent that Goebel and M. I. Hummel were major forces in the U.S. market.

In 1971 the company celebrated its one-hundredth anniversary. To commemorate this event, two major creations had been planned well in advance by Franz. One stands today at the entrance to the factory—a six-foot replica of the M. I. Hummel figurine, *Merry Wanderer*, a light-hearted invitation to visitors to come inside. Sculpted by master sculptor Gerhard Skrobek, it stands as a tribute to the worldwide appreciation of this line of figurines.

The second development was the issue of an annual plate. The collector plate market was in its infancy, with just a few companies producing them. Once the first edition M. I. Hummel plate, with Heavenly Angel as its motif, had been accepted by the public, plate collecting was on its way to becoming a major hobby. Within a few short years, the 1971 plate's initial price of $25 was spiraling upward with dizzying speed on the secondary market.

With more and more visitors coming to Roedental, and a seemingly endless number of rumors circulating among consumers and retailers (chief among them that the factory had burned down, which it never had!), Goebel management hit upon a novel idea. Perhaps there was a positive way to bring all these rumors to rest, and to respond to other pertinent questions. The decision was ultimately reached: it was time to start a club for collectors. Never before within the industry had such a concept been developed. Once again, the company demonstrated its originality and innovation.

The Club (whose history is detailed in Chapter IV) soon proved its worth. It was obvious that collectors were paying attention. Company representation in retail stores and at collector shows (which had become annual events within the industry) became a valuable learning tool. This program began with appearances of personnel from the Goebel Collectors' Club (since 1989 the M. I. Hummel Club), and eventually expanded to include demonstrations by decorators and sculptors from the company. In 1983 Goebel pioneered once again with its Facsimile Factory, which traveled to shopping malls throughout the United States, allowing the general public to "walk through the factory" to see, firsthand, the exciting process of handcrafting figurines. Applauded by the industry at large for its educational value, the Facsimile Factory was a great boon for collectors.

The company began to see a more knowledgeable collecting community. The growth of the secondary market, with the quest for older markings and variations, escalated. The marketing department, in close contact with the marketing and distributing factors in the United States, began to take closer note of trends and interests among collectors, and introduced previously unheard-of elements into the production of the figurines. Limited production pieces, some of them commemorative of specific events, began to appear, to the great pleasure of the collecting public.

By the late 1980s, it was clear that collecting of M. I. Hummel figurines was not only a North American phenomenon. Clusters of collectors had sprung up in Australia, Sweden, England, the Netherlands, Japan, and, of course, in West Germany itself. On the first of June, 1989, the International M. I. Hummel Club came into formal existence in Europe, with a strong plan for growth throughout the world.

The World Changes

The late 1980s began to bring worldwide political changes as well. Communism, once thought to be an indomitable and everlasting force throughout Eastern Europe and feared as a potential menace to the west, began to show signs of crumbling. Beginning to the east, in Poland, Czechoslovakia and Hungary, the rumblings soon reached into East Germany. On October 3, 1989, the unimaginable happened: the Berlin Wall began to crumble, as jubilant East Germans took picks, knives, hammers, hands—whatever was at the ready—to the bricks, and began to tear down the dreaded symbol.

Soon there was joyous chaos throughout Germany. The streets of Coburg were filled with cars showing East German license plates. Residents from across the border created heavy traffic jams by parking on the street, up the curb, wherever there was a space, looking for good food, clothing and other merchandise that had been unavailable to them for so long.

In late 1990, through a general election, the final political barriers were dismissed as the two Germanys ceased to be and, under one flag, a united Federal Republic of Germany came into being. Now, many of those who had been born in the Coburg area, or whose

Below:
The 1971 M. I. Hummel annual plate was one of the first collector plates to be issued, and helped to launch plate collecting as a popular hobby.

Bottom: This aerial view of the Facsimile Factory shows the progression visitors made, although we cannot see the sculptor, who would have been at the entranceway at the top of this picture. At the upper right is the moldmaker, next the assembler, the kiln for the bisque firing (at lower right, partially hidden), and the decorator at lower left. Visitors then went through the opening to the Information Center.

Jubilee, Hum 416, *was issued in 1985 to commemorate fifty years of the figurines, and is a popular gift for fiftieth wedding anniversaries or birthdays.*

families had come from there but who had been brutally torn away in the mid-1940s at the time of the division, could return just by an easy walk, bike ride or drive over the former border. Nearly two hundred are now working at Goebel, continuing their families' traditions in ceramic production.

Figurines Exemplify Life

The endurance of M. I. Hummel figurines is perhaps a tribute to all the history that has been made in the years since their inception: political turmoil, personal loss, the hope that remained in the hearts of the oppressed and the simple persistence of handcraftsmanship in a technological age. All of this, the unspeakable as well as the ordinary, has become part of life as it has been lived in the twentieth century.

M. I. Hummel figurines have not only helped to ease many people through the unrest and tragedies (both on a grand scale and within their personal daily lives), but have been part of the celebrations as well. They are viewed by collectors as part of life. It is not unusual for a collector to write that, after the death of a child, she was inconsolable until someone presented her with an M. I. Hummel figurine that directly related, in appearance or activity, to that child. In some form, therefore, she had her child again.

They commemorate specific events in peoples' lives. In 1985, to honor fifty years of the figurines, *Jubilee* (Hum 416) was produced. Countless collectors saw this figurine, with its flowers and its symbol of "50," as the perfect gift for a fiftieth wedding anniversary or birthday.

M. I. Hummel figurines represent life for those who hold them dear. They bring joy, they mark sadness, they speak of the cycle we all endure. They bring a closeness to the remarkable artist whose name they bear. For all those who understand, M. I. Hummel figurines will continue to "live" for many more years to come.

M. I. Hummel dolls are also popular collectibles; some wear authentic Bavarian costume and many represent actual figurines.

The stunning events in recent history that are changing the maps of the world serve to punctuate a fact known to countless numbers of collectors everywhere: no matter what the world looks like, M. I. Hummel figurines have a timelessness that prevails.

Although most of the designs for the figurines were drawn during the stressful period of the mid-1930s, the profound love and understanding of the innocence and playfulness of childhood that Sister Maria Innocentia portrayed so well are what shine through. These are children content among themselves, whether quietly reading a book, involved in a simple game with playmates, human and otherwise, or learning to be helpful around the house. They could be inhabitants of any time in history.

The pages of the M. I. Hummel Gallery point up this remarkable fact. Photographed with the utmost simplicity, the pictures emphasize the uncluttered qualities of the figurines themselves. It is no wonder that, to many people, these figurines exemplify children they knew when they themselves were children, or those they know today. Often, a figurine will commemorate a particular event in their own lives. These are ceramic portraits drawn from life; the subjects were frequently children who attended kindergarten at the Convent of Siessen and others from the nearby town of Saulgau, in Germany.

The combination of artistry is evident in every rendering. Each handcrafted figurine is faithful to the intent of the original drawing or painting, whether of an exuberant child or a serene portrayal of a religious figure. The acute sensibilities and talents of the sculptors and decorators who transform each two-dimensional sketch into the three-dimensional figurine are masterful in themselves. The sisters who comprise the board that convenes at the Convent to study each proposed piece, or change in an existing one, are mindful of their task to preserve the legacy that has been left to them. It is through this close association and the full acceptance of their individual responsibilities that the art of M. I. Hummel can continue to bring pleasure to its varied public.

This revised edition of the Golden Anniversary Album contains additional material developed from official Goebel records. It includes photography of all M. I. Hummel figurines, plates, bells and other renderings that have been authorized by the Convent of Siessen for production to date. Most have already been released by Goebel; some are scheduled for introduction beyond the publication date of this book.

Updated material has been added to this edition, including information on both permanently retired and temporarily withdrawn collectibles, as well as details of special and limited editions. A collectors' log has been added to the index, beginning on page 307, as an assist to the advanced collector.

Opposite page:
This rendering of Crossroads, HUM 331, *showing the "Halt" sign on the ground in commemoration of the opening of the East-West border in Germany, marked an unprecedented step. Created in 1990, it was the first M. I. Hummel figurine to be sequentially numbered in a limited edition. Only 20,000 pieces were produced for worldwide distribution.*

Above:
Pleasant Journey, Hum 406, *was released in 1987 as the second edition of the Century Collection. It is now a closed edition.*

Top:
Harmony in Four Parts, HUM
471, *was released in 1989 as the
fourth edition of the Century
Collection. These special issues
are not produced beyond the
year of release, and will never
be produced again in the twentieth century. Their special
backstamp exemplifies that. (See
page 275.)*

Above:
We Wish You the Best, HUM
600, *was released in 1991 as the
sixth edition of the Century Collection.*

Opposite page:
Let's Tell the World, HUM 487, the fifth edition of the Century Collection, was released in 1990. In commemoration of the tearing down of the Berlin Wall, a special bronze medallion was struck for the United States to accompany each figurine. The inscription reads: Let's Tell the World—Ringing in the Year of Freedom—1990.

Top:
On Our Way, HUM 472, *is scheduled for release in 1992 as the seventh edition of the Century Collection.*

Above: left to right:
On Holiday, HUM 350.
Little Hiker, HUM 16.
Chapel Time, HUM 442, *the first M. I. Hummel clock to be released, was the first edition in the Century Collection, issued in 1986.*
We Congratulate, HUM 220.

Below, left to right:
Angel Serenade, Hum 83.
Good Shepherd, Hum 42.
Lullaby, candleholder, Hum 24.
Angel Duet, candleholder, Hum 193.
Call to Worship, clock, Hum 441, *was the third edition in the Century Collection, issued in 1988. It is now a closed edition.*

Land in Sight, HUM 530, *the second figurine to be sequentially numbered and limited to 30,000 pieces worldwide, was released in 1991 to commemorate the 500th anniversary of the discovery of America.*

Top:
*This bronze medallion, shown
front and back, was struck to accompany* Land in Sight, Hum 530.

Above, left to right:
Latest News, HUM 184; Postman,
HUM 119.

Top:
Young Scholar, HUM 464.

Above, left to right:
Storybook Time, HUM 458.
Scamp, HUM 553.

Opposite page:
In the Orchard, HUM 461.

Below, *left to right*:
Will It Sting? HUM 450.
Tit for Tat, HUM 462.

Below, left to right:
Grandma's Girl, HUM 561.
Grandpa's Boy, HUM 562.
Come On! HUM 468. *Possible future edition.*

Below, left to right:
Where Shall I Go? HUM 465.
Possible future edition.
One For You, One For Me,
HUM 482.

Top, left to right:
Do Re Mi, HUM 466. *Possible future edition.*
In the Meadow, HUM 459.

Above, left to right:
Kindergartner, HUM 467.
Do Re Mi, HUM 466. *Possible future edition.*

Top, left to right:
Hosanna, HUM 480.
Sleep, Little One, Sleep, HUM
456. *Possible future edition*.

Above, left to right:
A Budding Maestro, HUM 477;
Winter Song, HUM 476; Hosanna, HUM 480; Sound the
Trumpet, HUM 457.

Opposite page:
Jubilee, HUM 416, *is now a
closed edition. It was issued in
1985 to commemorate fifty years
of M. I. Hummel figurines*.

Top, left to right:
Make A Wish, HUM 475; I'm
Here, HUM 478.

Above, left to right:
Gentle Care, HUM 474. *Possible
future edition.*
In the Orchard, HUM 461.
Possible future edition.

Opposite page, left to right:
Shepherd Boy, HUM 395.
Possible future edition.
Autumn Harvest, HUM 355.

Top:
Angelic Song, HUM 261.

Above, left to right:
Song of Praise, HUM 454; The
Accompanist, HUM 453.

Overleaf, left to right:
Starting Young, HUM 469.
Possible future edition.
Time Out, HUM 470. *Possible
future edition.*

Below, left to right:
Adoration, HUM 23; Heavenly
Protection, HUM 88; Holy Child,
HUM 70.

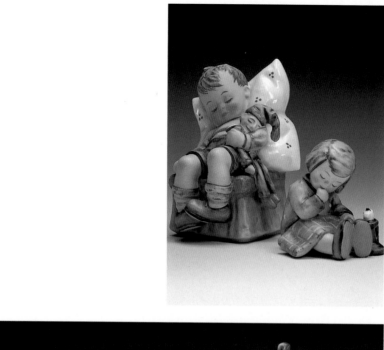

Top, left to right:
Just Dozing, HUM 451. *Possible future edition.*
A Nap, HUM 534.

Above, left to right:
I'll Protect Him, HUM 483;
The Guardian, HUM 455;
Evening Prayer, HUM 495.

Opposite page:
My Wish is Small, HUM 463.
Possible future edition.

Below, left to right:
Stormy Weather, HUM 71. Many
*size variations. First modeled
by Unger in 1937.*

March Winds, HUM 43. *Older
pieces slightly larger. Many size
variations.*

Below, left to right:
Globe Trotter, HUM 79.
Happy Traveler, HUM 109.

Below, left to right:
Umbrella Girl, HUM 152 B.
Modeled by Möller in 1949. Many
size variations. Crown mark
extremely rare.

Umbrella Boy, HUM 152 A. Crown
mark very rare.

Merry Wanderer, HUM 7. *First modeled by Möller in 1935. Can be found in more size variations than any other figurine. Some older models feature "stairstep" base. Restyled in 1972 with new textured finish.*

Below, left to right:
Bashful, HUM 377. *First released in United States in 1972.*

Soldier Boy, HUM 332. *First released in United States in 1963. Newer pieces have blue hat ornament; older pieces have red.*

Little Drummer, HUM 240. *First modeled by Unger in 1955.*

Volunteers, HUM 50. *First modeled by Unger in 1936.*

Surprise, HUM 94. *Older pieces have rectangular base. Newer pieces have oval base. First modeled in 1938.*

We Congratulate, HUM 220. *First modeled by Möller in 1952.*

Brother, HUM 95. *Many size and color variations. First modeled in 1938.*

Which Hand? HUM 258. *First modeled in 1962. First appeared in United States in 1964.*

Opposite page, top, left to right:
Wayside Harmony, HUM 111;
Crossroads, HUM 331; Little Hiker,
HUM 16; Home From Market,
HUM 198.

*Opposite page, bottom, left to
right:*
School Boy, HUM 82; Off To
School, HUM 329; Going To
Grandma's, HUM 52.

Top:
Smiling Through, HUM 408.
*Exclusive special edition for
Goebel Collectors' Club members
for 1985.*

Above, left to right:
Mountaineer, HUM 315; Farewell,
HUM 65; Little Cellist, HUM 89; The
Run-A-Way, HUM 327.

The Run-A-Way, HUM 327. Older trademarks considered rare.

Little Cellist, HUM 89. Modeled by Möller in 1938. Restyled in 1960's.

Strolling Along, HUM 5. *First modeled by Möller in 1935. Color of dog will vary.*

Auf Wiedersehen, HUM 153. *Restyled in recent years. Variation with boy wearing hat considered very rare.*

Top, left to right:
Good Luck! HUM 419 (*two views*). *Possible future edition.* Pleasant Journey, HUM 406, *is now a closed edition. It was the second edition in the Century Collection.*

Above, left to right:
Lucky Boy, HUM 335. *Possible future edition.*
Flower Vendor, HUM 381.

Opposite page:
Meditation, Hum 13.

Above:
Meditation, Hum 292, *is the first edition in the four-part series entitled Friends Forever. It is scheduled for introduction in 1992.*

Overleaf, left to right:
Flower Girl, HUM 548; I Brought You a Gift, HUM 479; I Wonder, HUM 486; Honey Lover, HUM 312; One Hand, One Treat, HUM 493; The Little Pair, HUM 449; Gift From A Friend, HUM 485. *These are some of the figurines created exclusively for members of the M. I. Hummel Club.*

Top, left to right:
To Market, HUM 49; Follow the Leader, HUM 369.

Above, left to right:
These are some of the exclusive collectibles created for the members of the Goebel Collectors' Club (since 1989, the M. I. Hummel Club).
What Now? HUM 422. *Seventh edition (1983–84).*
Coffee Break, HUM 409. *Eighth edition (1984–85).*
Valentine Gift, HUM 387. *First edition (1977–78).*
Valentine Joy, HUM 399. *Fourth edition (1980–81).*

Below, left to right:
It's Cold, HUM 421. *Special 1982*
Collectors' Club edition #6.

Daisies Don't Tell, HUM 380.
Collectors' Club edition #5 for
1981.

Below, left to right:
Happy Pastime, HUM 69; I Won't
Hurt You, HUM 428; Friend or Foe,
HUM 434. HUM 428 and HUM 434
are possible future editions.

True Friendship, HUM 402.
Modeled by Skrobek in 1973.
Possible future edition.

Top, left to right:
Honey Lover, HUM 312. *This
piece is an exclusive edition for
fifteen-year members of the
M. I. Hummel Club.*
Being Punished, Wall Plaque,
HUM 326. *Possible future edi-
tion.*

Above, left to right:
The Florist, HUM 349. *Possible
future edition.*
Honey Lover, HUM 312.

Top, left to right:
Max and Moritz, HUM 123;
Congratulations, HUM 17.

Above, left to right:
Smart Little Sister, HUM 346;
Carnival, HUM 328; Star Gazer,
HUM 132.

Opposite page, left to right:
Gay Adventure, HUM 356;
Trumpet Boy, HUM 97.

Below, left to right:
Out of Danger, HUM 56B.
Modeled by Möller in 1952.
Variation in height and size of
base.

Culprits, HUM 56A. *Modeled by*
Möller in 1936. Restyled in later
years. Restyled pieces have extra
branch by boy's feet.

Below, left to right:
Apple Tree Boy, HUM 142.
Modeled by Möller in 1940.
Restyled many times over the
years. Many size variations.
Smaller models made without bird
in tree.

Apple Tree Girl, HUM 141. *Modeled*
by Möller in 1940. Restyled many
times over the years. Many size
variations. Smaller models made
without bird in tree.

Above, left to right:
Where Did You Get That?
Hum 417.
Do I Dare? Hum 411. *Possible future edition.*

Above, left to right:
An Apple A Day, HUM 403.
Whistlers' Duet, HUM 413.
Well Done! HUM 400.
Possible future edition.

Top, left to right:
At The Fence, HUM 324.
Possible future edition.
Behave! HUM 339. *Possible future edition.*
Not For You! HUM 317.

Above, left to right:
Coquettes, HUM 179.
At The Fence, HUM 324.
Possible future edition.
Feathered Friends, HUM 344.

Opposite page, left to right:
Singing Lesson, HUM 63; Timid Little Sister, HUM 394.

She Loves Me, She Loves Me Not!
HUM 174. *Modeled by Möller in 1945. Restyled several times.*

Sensitive Hunter, HUM 6; *Friends,* HUM 136; *Good Hunting!* HUM 307; *Retreat to Safety,* HUM 201.

Mischief Maker, HUM 342; *Just Resting,* HUM 112; *Chicken-Licken!* HUM 385.

Book Ends: Little Goat Herder, HUM 250A; *Feeding Time,* HUM 250B; *Apple Tree Girl,* HUM 252A; *Apple Tree Boy,* HUM 252B.

Shepherd's Boy, HUM 64; *Lost Sheep,* HUM 68; *Good Friends,* HUM 182; *Little Goat Herder,* HUM 200; *Favorite Pet,* HUM 361; *Just Resting,* HUM 112.

Barnyard Hero, HUM 195; *Goose Girl,* HUM 47; *Be Patient,* HUM 197; *Playmates,* HUM 58; *Easter Time,* HUM 384; *Farm Boy,* HUM 66.

Don't Be Shy, HUM 379; *Companions,* HUM 370; *Daddy's Girls,* HUM 371; *Just Fishing,* HUM 373; *The Botanist,* HUM 351; *Lute Song,* HUM 368.

Top, left to right:
Chick Girl, HUM 57; Feeding
Time, HUM 199.

Above, left to right:
Sister, HUM 98; Easter Greet-
ings, HUM 378; Little Shopper,
HUM 96.

Opposite page:
Cinderella, HUM 337.

Feathered Friends, HUM 344.

Top, left to right,
Book Ends:
Playmates, HUM 61A; Chick
Girl, HUM 61B.
Above, left to right,
Book Ends:
Goose Girl, HUM 60B; Farm
Boy, HUM 60A.
These four book ends were tem-
porarily withdrawn in December
1984.

Top, left to right,
Book Ends:
Good Friends, HUM 251A; She
Loves Me, She Loves Me Not!
HUM 251B.

Above, left to right:
Sing With Me, HUM 405.
Forty Winks, HUM 401. *Possible*
future edition.
Flute Song, HUM 407. *Possible*
future edition.
Spring Bouquet, HUM 398.
Possible future edition.

In Tune, HUM 414. *Modeled by Skrobek in 1979. Released in United States in 1981.*

Below, left to right:
School Boys, HUM 170; School
Girls, HUM 177.

Above, left to right:
Book Worm, HUM 3; Thoughtful, HUM 415; Book Worm, HUM 3 (*rear view*), Busy Student, HUM 367; Mother's Helper, HUM 133.
Some sizes of Book Worm, Hum 3, *were temporarily withdrawn in January 1989.*

Opposite page, left to right:
What's New? HUM 418.
The Poet, HUM 397. *Possible future edition.*

Below, left to right:
Book Worm, HUM 3. Book Worm, *Book End, Boy,* HUM 14A. Book Worm, *Book End, Girl,* HUM 14B. Book Worm, *Book End, Girl,* HUM 14B *(rear view).*

Top, left to right:
Little Scholar, HUM 80.
Arithmetic Lesson, HUM 303.
Possible future edition.
School Girl, HUM 81. *Two sizes shown.*

Above, left to right:
The Professor, HUM 320;
School Boy, HUM 82.

Below, left to right:
Is It Raining? HUM 420. *Modeled by Skrobek in 1981. Possible future edition.*

Truant, HUM 410. *Modeled by Skrobek in 1978. Possible future edition.*

Country Song, *Clock*, HUM 443.

Top, left to right:
The Builder, HUM 305; Little
Thrifty, Bank, HUM 118.

Above, left to right:
Chimney Sweep, HUM 12 (*two
views shown*); Mother's Darling,
HUM 175.

Below, left to right:
Sister, HUM 98; Little Shopper,
HUM 96; On Holiday, HUM
350; Sweet Greetings, HUM 352;
Little Sweeper, HUM 171.

Bottom:
Big Housecleaning, HUM 363.

Opposite page:
Wash Day, HUM 321.

Happy Birthday, HUM 176.
Modeled by Möller in 1945.
Restyled in 1979 with oval base.
Old model had round base.

Going to Grandma's, HUM 52.
Modeled in 1936 by Unger.

Objects inside cone represent
candy and sweets, not flowers.
Cone appears empty on large
models. Restyled in 1960's and in
1979. Crown marks considered
rare.

Begging His Share, HUM 9.
Modeled by Möller in 1935. Many size variations. Restyled in 1964 without hole for candle in cake. Old models have brightly colored striped socks.

Above, left to right:
Boots, HUM 143 (*two views shown*); Weary Wanderer, HUM 204; Lost Stocking, HUM 374.

Opposite page:
For Father, HUM 87.

Below, left to right:
Baker, HUM 128. Modeled by Möller in 1939. Restyled several times, most recently in the mid-1970's with textured finish.

Hello, HUM 124. Many size variations. Many color variations in coat, trousers and vest. Crown marks are considered rare.

Waiter, HUM 154. First produced with gray coat and gray-striped trousers. Now has blue coat and tan-striped trousers. Various names used on bottle, most prominent being "Rhein Wine." Crown mark considered rare.

Accordian Boy, HUM 185 *(reverse angle view).*

Little Bookkeeper, HUM 306. *Modeled in 1955 by Möller. Introduced in United States in 1962. Full bee mark considered rare.*

A Fair Measure, HUM 345. *Full bee mark considered rare.*

Below, left to right:
Little Pharmacist, HUM 322.
*Introduced in United States in
1962. Variations on bottle name,
mostly "Rizinusöl," or "Vitamins."
Full bee mark rare.*

Boy With Toothache, HUM 217.
Modeled by Möller in 1951.

Below, left to right:
Little Nurse, HUM 376. *Released in United States in 1982.*

Doctor, HUM 127. *Modeled by Möller in 1939. Has been restyled with textured finish.*

Above, left to right:
An Emergency, HUM 436.
Possible future edition.
Pleasant Moment, HUM 425.
Possible future edition.
Sing Along, HUM 433.

Opposite page, left to right:
Spring Cheer, HUM 72; Confi-
dentially, HUM 314; Little Gar-
dener, HUM 74.

Below, left to right:
Sunny Morning, HUM 313.
Modeled by Möller in 1955.
Possible future edition.

I Forgot, HUM 362. *Possible future*
edition.

Relaxation, HUM 316. *Possible*
future edition.

Morning Stroll, HUM 375.
Modeled by Skrobek in 1964.
Possible future edition.

Below, left to right:
Girl With Doll, HUM 239B; Boy
With Horse, HUM 239C; Prayer
Before Battle, HUM 20; Girl
With Nosegay, HUM 239A.

Bottom:
Horse Trainer, HUM 423.

Below, left to right:
Doll Mother, HUM 67; Blessed Event, HUM 333; Stitch In Time, HUM 255; Happy Pastime, HUM 69; Little Tailor, HUM 308; Knitting Lesson, HUM 256; Doll Bath, HUM 319; Kiss Me, HUM 311.

Below, left to right:
The Tuba Player, HUM 437; In
D-Major, HUM 430. Both are
possible future editions.

Above, left to right:
Sad Song, HUM 404. *Possible
future edition.*
Morning Concert, HUM 447.
*This figurine was the eleventh
edition created exclusively for
members of the Goebel Collectors' Club (now the M. I. Hummel club) in 1987–1988.*

Serenade, HUM 85. *Modeled by Möller in 1938. Recently restyled with textured finish. Some variations in color of hat. Crown marks considered rare.*

Band Leader, HUM 129. *Modeled by Möller in 1939.*

Duet, HUM 130 *(rear view).*

Below, left to right:
Let's Sing, HUM 110. *Modeled by Unger in 1938.*

Joyful, HUM 53. *Modeled by Unger in 1936. Some early crown mark pieces have orange dress and blue shoes, considered rare. Current models have a brown-colored mandolin.*

Close Harmony, HUM 336.

Birthday Serenade, HUM 218. *Modeled by Unger in 1952. Remodeled in 1964 by Skrobek.*

exist.

Girl With Sheet of Music, HUM 389. *Modeled by Skrobek in 1968.*

Birthday Serenade, HUM 218.

Boy With Accordian, HUM 390. *Modeled by Skrobek in 1968.*

Girl With Trumpet, HUM 391. *Modeled by Skrobek in 1968.*

Above, left to right:
Puppy Love, HUM 1. *This figu-*
rine was permanently retired in
1988.
Little Fiddler, HUM 4; Little
Cellist, HUM 89.

Opposite page:
Sweet Music, HUM 186.

Little Fiddler, HUM 2. Modeled by
Möller in 1935. Large crown mark
and full bee pieces considered rare.

Ring Around the Rosie, HUM 348.
Modeled by Skrobek in 1957.
Full bee pieces very rare. Stylized
pieces also rare.

Opposite page, left to right,
Table Lamps:
Culprits, HUM 44A; Birthday
Serenade, HUM 234; Happy Days,
HUM 232; Apple Tree Girl, HUM
229; She Loves Me, She Loves Me
Not! HUM 227.

This page, left to right:
To Market, *Table Lamp,* HUM 223;
Little Band, *Candle Holder on
Music Box,* HUM 388M.

Top, left to right:
Candleholders:
Joyous News (*Lute*), HUM 38;
Joyous News (*Accordion*), HUM
39; Joyous News (*Trumpet*),
HUM 40.

Above, left to right:
Candlesticks:
Good Friends, HUM 679; Apple
Tree Boy, HUM 677; Apple Tree
Girl, HUM 676; She Loves Me,
She Loves Me Not! HUM 678.

Top:
Out of Danger, *Lamp*, HUM
44B. *This piece was temporarily
withdrawn in January 1990.*

*Above, left to right,
Table Lamps:*
Apple Tree Boy, HUM 230;
Good Friends, HUM 228; Just
Resting, HUM 225; Wayside Har-
mony, HUM 224. *These pieces
were all temporarily withdrawn
in January 1990.*

Above, left to right:
Skier, HUM 59; Letter to Santa
Claus, HUM 340.

Opposite page:
Ride Into Christmas, HUM 396.

Below, left to right:
With Loving Greetings, HUM 309.
Released in United States in 1983.

Birthday Present, HUM 341.
Possible future edition.

Knit One, Purl One, HUM 432.
Modeled by Skrobek in 1982.

Helping Mother, HUM 325. *Possible future edition.*

Birthday Cake, HUM 338. *Possible future edition.*

Concentration, HUM 302. *Possible future edition.*

Baking Day, HUM 330. *To be released in the United States in 1985.*

Little Helper, HUM 73. *Modeled in 1937 by Unger.*

Top, left to right:
Girl With Nosegay, Advent Candlestick, HUM 115; Angel With Accordian, HUM 238B; Boy With Horse, Advent Candlestick, HUM 117; Angel With Lute, HUM 238A; Heavenly Lullaby, HUM 262; Angelic Song, HUM 144; Girl With Fir Tree, Advent Candlestick, HUM 116; Angel With Trumpet, HUM 238C.

Above, left to right:
Christmas Song, HUM 343.
Watchful Angel, HUM 194.
Littlest Angel, HUM 365. *Possible future edition.*
Christmas Angel, HUM 301.

Opposite page, left to right:
Lamb from Nativity Set, HUM 214/0.
Angel Serenade, HUM 260E.
Blessed Child, HUM 78. *Some sizes of this piece have been temporarily withdrawn.*

Opposite page:
Angel Lights, Candleholder,
HUM 241. *This piece has been
temporarily withdrawn.*

Below, left to right:
Joyous News, HUM 27; Festival
Harmony (*Flute*), HUM 173; Festival Harmony (*Mandolin*), HUM
172; Christ Child, HUM 18; Can-
dlelight, Candleholder, HUM
192; Celestial Musician, HUM
188; Heavenly Angel, HUM 21.

Opposite page, left to right:
Birthday Candle, HUM 440. *This piece was the tenth edition created for members of the Goebel Collectors' Club, now the M. I. Hummel Club, in 1986–87.*
Well Done! HUM 400. *Possible future edition.*

Top, left to right:
Sounds of the Mandolin, HUM 438; A Gentle Glow, HUM 439, Sounds of the Mandolin, HUM 438.

Above, left to right:
Angel Duet, *Candleholder*, HUM 193; Angelic Sleep, *Candleholder*, HUM 25; Little Gabriel, HUM 32.

Nativity Set with Wooden Stable,
HUM 214.
Flying Angel, HUM 366.
This nativity set was modeled by Unger in 1951, and first produced and sold in 1952. It is also available in individual pieces.

At one time this set was produced and sold in white overglaze finish, but it is no longer sold this way. The white overglaze finish is considered rare. Early production of HUM 214A (Virgin Mary and Infant Jesus) was made in one piece. Because of production problems, it was later produced as two separate pieces, both with the same number (214A) incised in the bottom of each piece. Two different styles of lambs (214/0) have been used with the Nativity sets.

Some Nativity set pieces have an incised 1951 copyright date. Wooden stable is usually sold separately. The sixteenth piece, Flying Angel, HUM 366, was added to the set in 1963.

Large Nativity Set With Wooden
Stable, HUM 260. *Modeled in 1968
by Skrobek: Various types of
wooden stables have been used
over the years.*

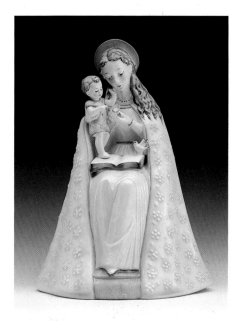

Above:
Flower Madonna, HUM 10.

Opposite page:
Supreme Protection, HUM 364.
This figurine was produced only in 1984 in honor of the 75th anniversary of Sister Maria Innocentia Hummel's birth. It is now a closed edition.

Below, left to right:
Madonna Holding Child, HUM
151; Flower Madonna, HUM 10.

Bottom, left to right:
Madonna Without Halo, HUM 46.
Blessed Mother, HUM 372.
Possible future edition.
Madonna With Halo, HUM 45.

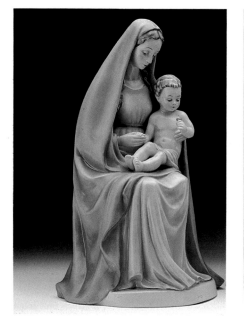

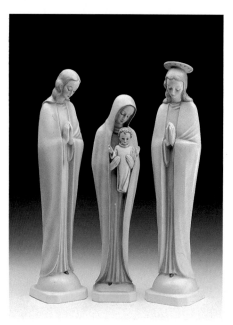

Top, left to right:
Children's Prayer, HUM 448.
Possible future edition.
Pay Attention, HUM 426.
Possible future edition.
Hello World, HUM 429, *was the twelfth edition created exclusively for members of the M. I. Hummel Club in 1988–89.*
The Surprise, HUM 431, *was the thirteenth edition created exclusively for members of the M. I. Hummel Club, in 1989–90.*
Where Are You? HUM 427.
Possible future edition.

Above, left to right:
On Secret Path, HUM 386; Bird Watcher, HUM 300; Forest Shrine, HUM 183; Eventide, HUM 99; On Secret Path, HUM 386 (*rear view*).

Opposite page, left to right:
Village Boy, HUM 51; For Mother, HUM 257; Girl With Nosegay, HUM 239A; Worship, HUM 84; For Mother, HUM 257.

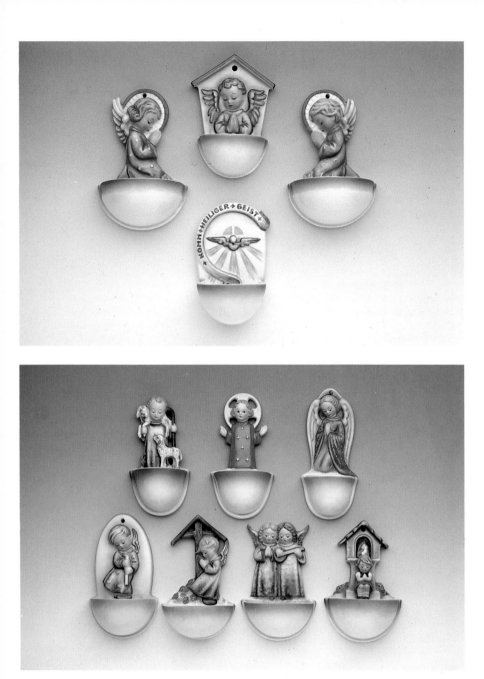

Top, left to right,
Holy Water Fonts:
Angel Facing Right, HUM 91B.
White Angel, HUM 75. Dove,
HUM 393. Possible future edition. Angel Facing Left, HUM
91A.

Center, top row, left to right,
Holy Water Fonts:
Good Shepherd, HUM 35;
Child Jesus, HUM 26; Guardian
Angel, HUM 248.
Center, bottom row, left to
right,
Holy Water Fonts:
Heavenly Angel, HUM 207;
Angel Shrine, HUM 147; Angel
Duet, HUM 146; Worship, HUM
164.

Bottom, top row, left to right,
Holy Water Fonts:
Angel With Birds, HUM 22;
Madonna And Child, HUM 243;
Holy Family, HUM 246.
Bottom, bottom row, left to
right,
Holy Water Fonts:
Child With Flowers, HUM 36;
Angel Sitting, HUM 167;
Angel Cloud, HUM 206.

Opposite page:
Madonna Plaque, HUM 48. This
piece was temporarily withdrawn in December 1989.

Top, left to right,
Holy Water Fonts:
Joyous News with Trumpet,
HUM 242. *Closed number;*
never produced.
Guardian Angel, HUM 29.
Closed edition.
Joyous News with Lute, HUM
241. *Closed number; never produced.*

Above, left to right,
Holy Water Fonts:
Angel with Lantern, HUM 354A.
Closed number; never produced.
Angel with Trumpet, HUM 354B.
Closed number; never produced.
Angel with Bird, HUM 354C.
Closed number; never produced.

Above, left to right,
Annual Ornaments:
Flying High, HUM 452, 1988;
Love From Above, HUM 481,
1989; Angelic Guide, HUM 571,
1991; Light Up the Night, HUM
622, 1992; Peace On Earth, HUM
484, 1990.

Opposite page, left to right,
Wall Plaques:
Searching Angel, HUM 310;
Merry Christmas, HUM 323.

*Top, top row, left to right,
Ornaments*:
Angel in Cloud, HUM 585;
Angel with Trumpet, HUM 586.
*Top, center row, left to right,
Ornaments*:
Angel with Flute, HUM 582;
Praying Angel, HUM 581; Celestial Musician, HUM 578; Heavenly Angel, HUM 575.
*Top, bottom row, left to right,
Ornaments*:
Festival Harmony (flute), HUM 577; Festival Harmony (mandolin), HUM 576; Song of Praise, HUM 579; Angel with Lute, HUM 580.

*Above, top row, left to right,
Unnumbered Christmas plates*:
Celestial Musician; Angel Duet.
*Above, bottom row, left to right,
Unnumbered Christmas plates*:
Christmas Song; Tender Watch.

Top, left to right,
Four Seasons Music Boxes:
Summer, In Tune, 1989; Spring,
Chick Girl, 1988.

Center, left to right,
Four Seasons Music Boxes:
Fall, Umbrella Girl, 1990; Winter,
Ride Into Christmas, 1987.

Bottom, left to right, Bookends,
all factory samples only:
Doll Mother, HUM 76A; Even-
ide, HUM 90A; Adoration,
HUM 90B.

Above left:
Flitting Butterfly, *Wall Plaque,* HUM 139.

Center, left to right:
Ba-Bee Ring, HUM 30A; Ba-Be
Ring, HUM 30B.

Below left:
Child in Bed, *Wall Plaque,* HUM
137.

Opposite page:
Swaying Lullaby, *Wall Plaque,*
HUM 165. *This piece was temporarily withdrawn in Decembe
1989.*

Er träumt von besseren Zeiten

Top, left to right,
Wall Plaques:
Merry Wanderer, HUM 92; Little Fiddler, HUM 93; Retreat to Safety, HUM 126.

Above, clockwise, from right to left,
Wall Plaques: ›
Quartet, HUM 134; Standing Boy, HUM 168; Vacation Time, HUM 125; The Mail Is Here, HUM 140.

All the wall plaques on this page have been temporarily withdrawn, excepting Quartet, HUM 134.

Right, top to bottom,
Anniversary Plates:
Stormy Weather, HUM 280, *1975*; Auf Wiedersehen HUM 282, *1985*; Spring Dance, HUM 281, *1980*. This series ended in *1985*.

Top, left to right,
Annual Bells:
Let's Sing, HUM 700, *1978*; Farewell, HUM 701, *1979*; In Tune, HUM 703, *1981*; Thoughtful, HUM 702, *1980*; She Loves Me, HUM 704, *1982*; Knit One, HUM 705, *1983*.

Above, left to right,
Annual Bells:
Mountaineer, HUM 706, *1984*; Sweet Song, HUM 707, *1985*; Sing Along, HUM 708, *1986*; With Loving Greetings, HUM 709, *1987*; Busy Student, HUM 710, *1988*; Latest News, HUM 711, *1989*; What's New? HUM 712, *1990*.

Right, left to right,
Annual Bells:
Favorite Pet, HUM 713, *1991*; Whistlers' Duet, HUM 714, *1992*. *This fifteen-year series will end in 1992.*

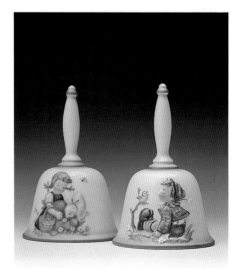

Annual plates, 1971–1992.
For HUM numbers and names,
see Plate section of index.

Top, left to right,
Christmas Bells:
Ride Into Christmas, HUM 775,
1989; Letter to Santa Claus,
HUM 776, *1990;* Hear Ye, Hear
Ye, HUM 777, *1991;* Harmony in
Four Parts, HUM 778, *1992. Each*
piece in this series was produced
for one year only.

Above and left:
These are the last three annual
plates of the twenty-five-year
series.

Left, right to left,
Kitchen molds:
For Father, HUM 672; Supper's
Coming, HUM 673; Baker,
HUM 674.

Right, left to right,
Kitchen molds:
Sweet As Can Be, HUM 671; A
Fair Measure, HUM 670; Baking
Day, HUM 669.

Left, left to right,
Wall vases:
Boy, HUM 360B; Boy/Girl, HUM
360A; HUM 360C, Girl. *These
pieces were all temporarily withdrawn in January 1990.*

*Opposite page and above:
Two series are uniquely displayed. These 3½-inch-high figurines are from* Little Music Makers *(Little Fiddler, HUM 2/4/0, Serenade, HUM 85/4/0, Soloist, HUM 135/4/0 and Band Leader, HUM 129/4/0). The figurines in the series* Little Homemakers *stand 3 inches high (Little Sweeper, HUM 171/4/0, Wash Day, HUM 321/4/0, Stitch in Time, HUM 255/4/0 and Chicken-Licken, HUM 385/4/0). Each matching plate was produced for one year only. The plates for* Little Music Makers *were dated 1984–1987; those for* Little Homemakers *were dated 1988–1991.*

*Overleaf:
Kinderway may be the smallest Bavarian village on record; these M. I. Hummel figurine miniatures are barely ⅞ inches high. Each is handcrafted in the ancient "lost wax" method. First it is sculpted in wax, then a plaster mold is made and the wax within melted out. Molten bronze is poured into the plaster mold which, once cooled, is then broken away to free the bronze. Each piece is then prepared for handpainting.*

Kinderway made its debut with its first inhabitants in 1988. By 1991 the village had grown to its present number. Shown here, left to right, are: Little Fiddler *(above), Doll Bath, Stormy Weather, Little Sweeper, Merry Wanderer, Apple Tree Boy, Cinderella, Waiter, Baker, Visiting an Invalid, Postman, Busy Student, Serenade, Accordion Boy, We Congratulate, plaque.*

Top, left to right:
M. I. Hummel porcelain dolls:
Friend or Foe? HUM 514; Goose
Girl, HUM 517.

Above, left to right:
M. I. Hummel porcelain dolls:
Umbrella Girl, HUM 512; Um-
brella Boy, HUM 518.

Top,
M. I. Hummel porcelain doll:
Ride Into Christmas, HUM 519.

Above,
M. I. Hummel porcelain dolls:
Merry Wanderer, HUM 516; Lit-
tle Fiddler, HUM 513.

Top, back row, left to right, Boxes:
Playmates, HUM III/58; Singing Lesson, HUM III/63; Let's Sing, HUM III/110.
Top, front row, left to right, Boxes:
Joyful, HUM III/53; Happy Pastime, HUM III/69; Chick Girl, HUM III/57.

Above, top row, left to right, Ashtrays:
Singing Lesson, HUM 34; Boy With Bird, HUM 166.
Above, bottom row, left to right, Ashtrays:
Let's Sing, HUM 114; Happy Pastime, HUM 62; Joyful, HUM 33.
All the pieces on this page have been temporarily withdrawn in December 1989 (top photo) and in December 1984 (above).

Above, left to right:
Coquettes, HUM 179; The Artist, HUM 304.

Below, left to right:
Photographer, HUM 178.

Adventure Bound, The Seven
Swabians, HUM 347. *Introduced in
United States in 1971.*

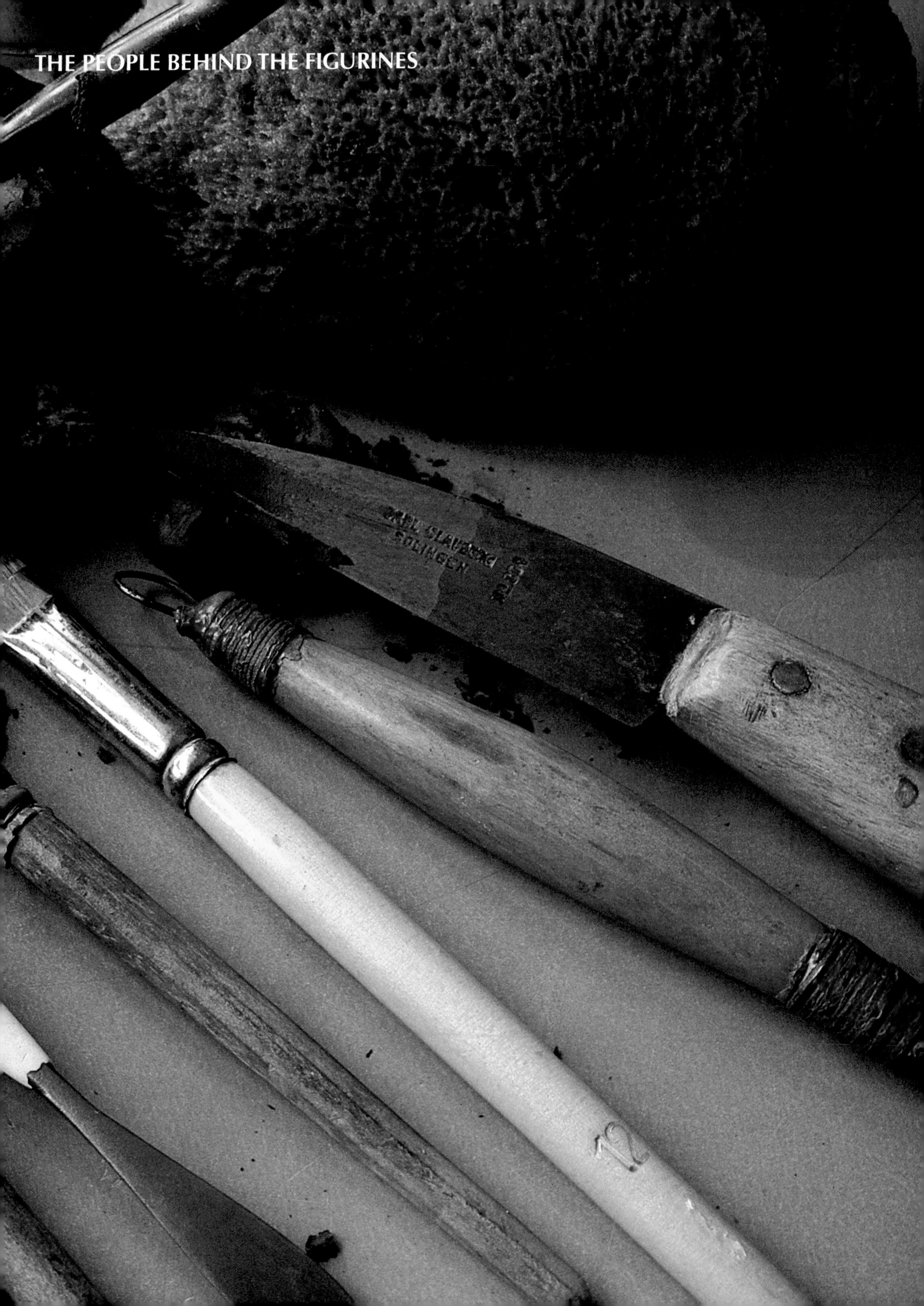
SOLINGEN

The tradition of fine handcraftsmanship evident in M. I. Hummel figurines is generations-old. For thousands of years, craftsmen have been creating ceramic figurines; in Europe, the tradition has flourished for hundreds of years. One of the cradles of figurine creation in Europe was central Germany, especially the famed factories of Meissen and Dresden. Not far from this celebrated ceramic center, in northeast Bavaria, is the Goebel factory, founded in 1871.

A tradition started is one thing. To uphold that tradition requires dedication. For generations, Goebel has maintained a rigorous apprentice program. The concept, dating back to the early days of the factory, was formalized in 1950. Whether it be studying with a master on the factory premises, or taking class at the ceramic college in nearby Selb, classroom assignments lead to reality for the teenagers who have been accepted into the program.

Credentials of the masters have always been high. The two who were the first to sculpt M. I. Hummel figurines, Arthur Moeller and Reinhold Unger, came to Goebel in 1911 and 1915, respectively. Behind them were their years of formal schooling: for Moeller, the Arts and Crafts Academy in Dresden and the Munich Academy of Applied Art (later attended by Berta Hummel prior to, and then during, her years in the Convent). Unger studied in Lichte, at the Fine Art School of Professor Hutschenreuther and subsequently worked at the art institute, the *Kunstanstalt Gaigl*, in Munich.

When Gerhard Skrobek joined the firm in 1951, he brought with him his years of study at Berlin's famous center for art studies, the *Reimannschule*, and his work in Coburg with the renowned sculptor Poertzel. Now that Gerhard Skrobek is retiring, the mantle of the sculpting of M. I. Hummel figurines is being passed, most notably to Helmut Fischer, who entered the apprentice program at the age of fourteen in 1964.

While sculpting is the beginning of a figurine, there are many vital steps along the way to completion, particularly capturing in ceramic the coloring so special to the original art of M. I. Hummel. Chief Master Sample Painter Guenther Neubauer, who became an apprentice at the age of sixteen in 1948 and rose to head a large section of the painting department by the age of twenty-one, was a talent recognized at an early age. Today he continues the tradition through his direct concerns with the current apprentices.

Many of those pictured on the following pages are carrying on their own traditions, for it is not unusual to find more than one generation of a family working side by side within the factory. This continuity brings with it the pride of workmanship and the dedication to quality. The combination yields the specialness of M. I. Hummel figurines, leading them to continue to be sought after among collectors the world over. The ultimate exemplification of this is the distinctive backstamp on the base—the Goebel mark.

Right: The birth of an M. I. Hummel figurine begins with a simple lump of clay.

Overleaf: Master Sculptor Helmut Fischer works on HUM 3, Book Worm, in his studio. The figurines are developed from color prints of Sister Maria Innocentia's artwork that have been published as art cards or as illustrations in children's books.

Second overleaf: The gentle configurations of a child's face are skillfully brought to life by the hands of the Master Sculptor.

Left: Master Sculptor Gerhard Skrobek and Master Moldmaker Florian Brechelmacher must decide into how many pieces Ride Into Christmas *will be cut for moldmaking purposes. Because of their detail, the figurines cannot be molded in one piece. The sculptor bears this in mind as he works.*

Top and above: Brechelmacher cuts Ride Into Christmas *into twelve pieces for moldmaking. A high degree of artistic excellence is required for this step.*

Left: The twelve separate pieces of Ride Into Christmas *include even the tiny candle that the boy holds. Because of the amount of detail, some of the larger figurines require as many as forty separate molds.*

Above: The first step after the clay model has been cut is to create the mother mold.

Overleaf: Liquid plaster of paris is poured over the model, held in by a plastic sheath. When the plaster dries, the mother mold is created.

Left to right: The plaster covers the clay piece to create the mother, or master, mold. After a series of positive and negative molds, the acrylic resin working model is created. The use of acrylic resin was pioneered in 1954 by a team of Goebel ceramic experts and improved this step in production. Until then, the expansion and loss of detail (often called "mold growth") in the mold, caused by the liquid in the plaster of paris was commonplace.

Overleaf: The acrylic resin working model, from which the working mold will be cast, is the dark form at the bottom right. The cream-colored form at left is the mother mold. At the upper right can be seen the formed head and torso of the boy, as the liquid ceramic slip has taken shape in the working mold.

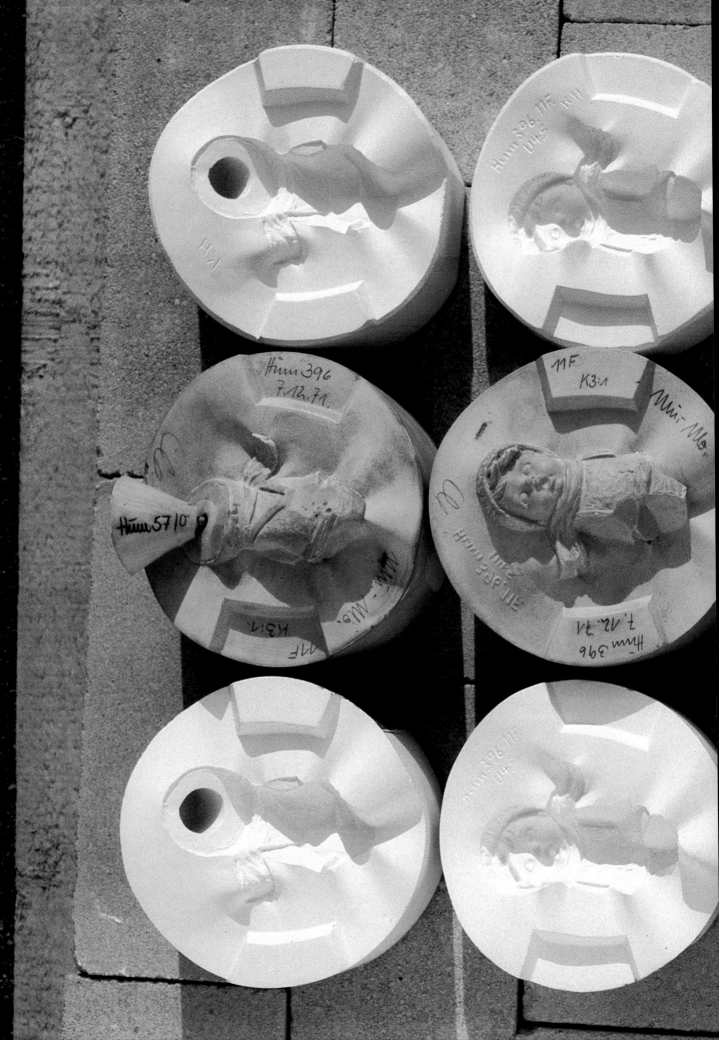

Below: The block and case working molds, from which the parts of the figurine are cast, lock into each other to form the mold. These molds can be used only a limited number of times before losing their detail. From each acrylic resin working model, identical new working molds are made. Because of this complexity, moldmaking is one of the major jobs at the factory.

Right: The number of plaster of paris working molds is marked in chalk on an old-time black-board, just as it was more than fifty years ago.

Overleaf: These twenty-four pieces comprise the set of plaster of paris working molds that cast the twelve parts of Ride Into Christmas. Each piece has its own number as well as HUM 396 incised on its surface.

Second overleaf: Liquid ceramic slip, finely ground at the factory, is composed of kaolin, quartz, clay, feldspar and water. Here a caster pours the slip into a working mold to cast a doll's head.

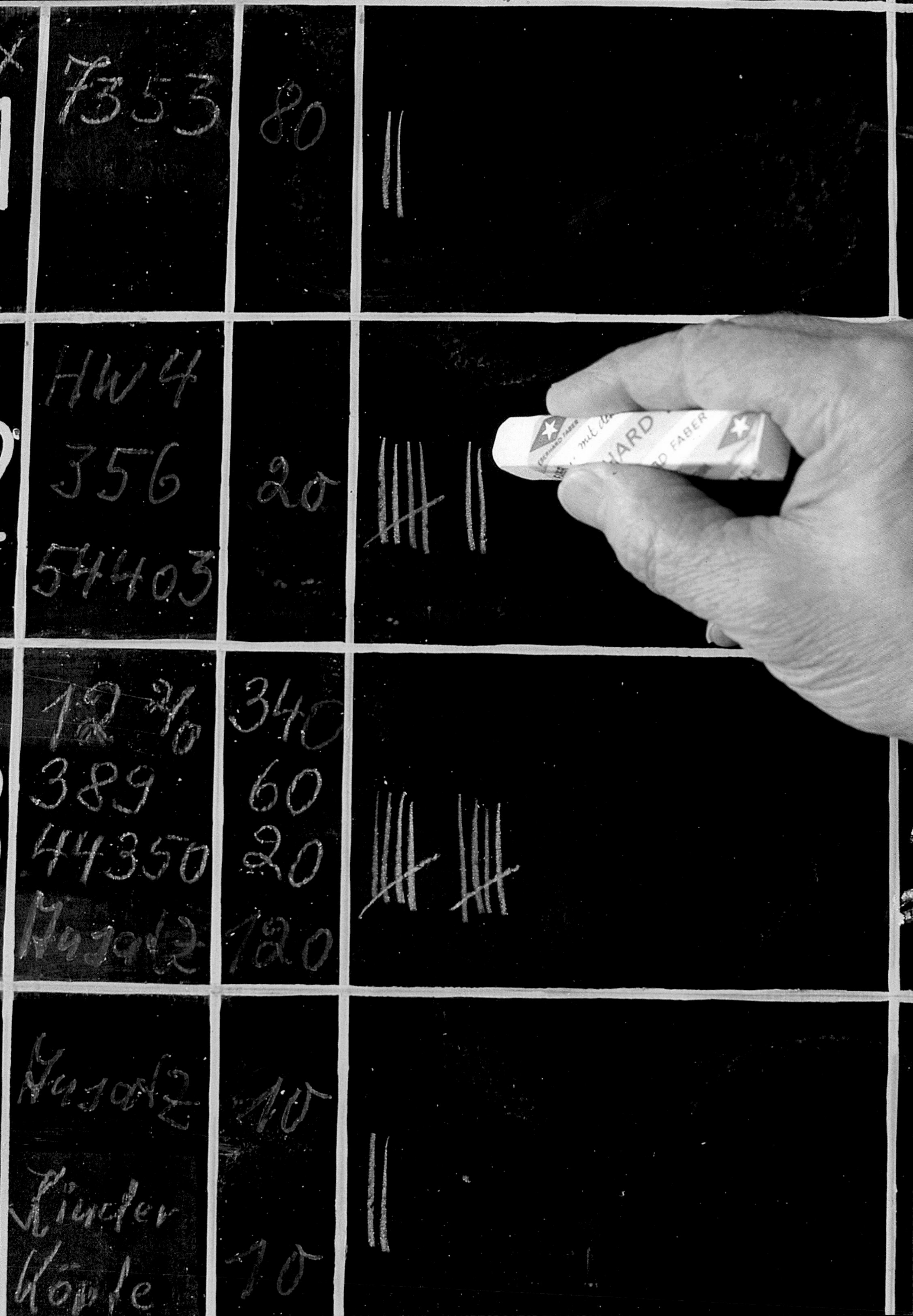

F353 80 ||

HW4

356 20 |||| ||

54403

12% 340

389 60

44350 20 |||| ||||

120

10

Kinder 10 ||

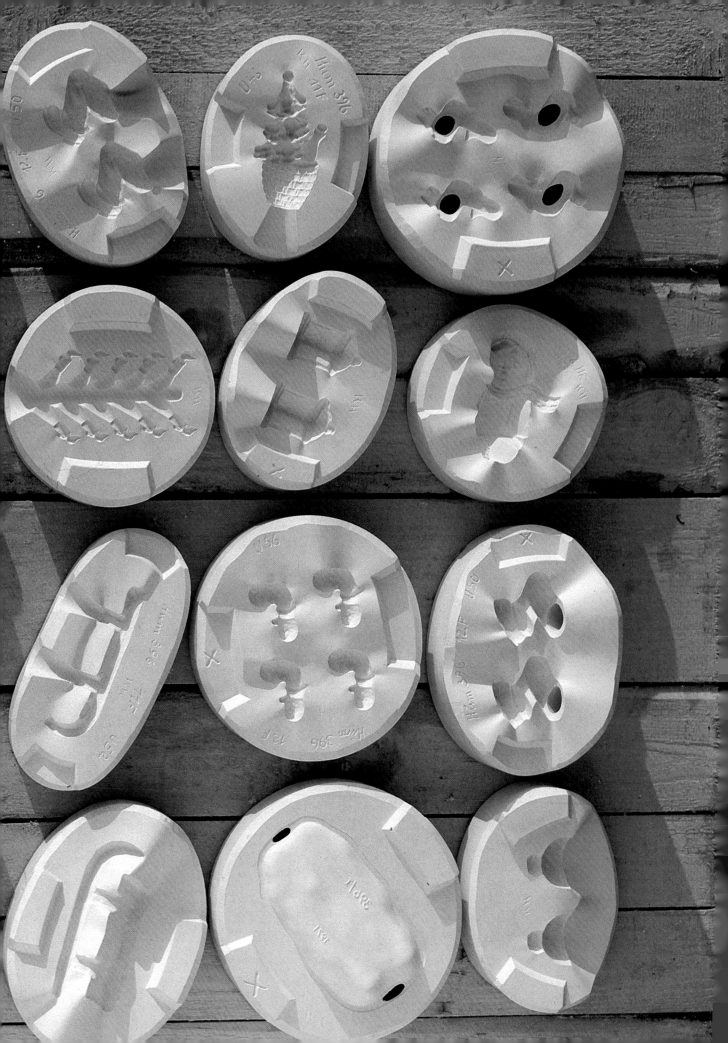

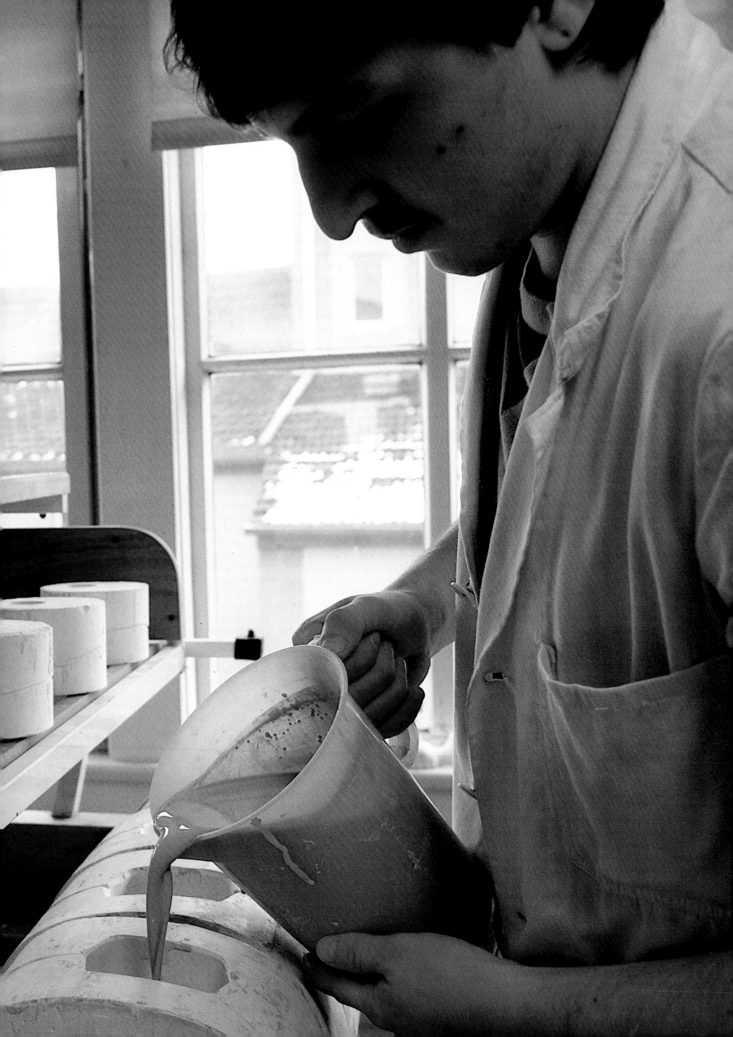

Left to right: The slip is poured into the mold. The ceramic is designed to withstand the high temperatures in the kiln.

The formula is monitored constantly by quality control experts in the laboratory. The amount of time the slip remains in the mold is timed carefully so that the actual part being cast will form to the desired consistency.

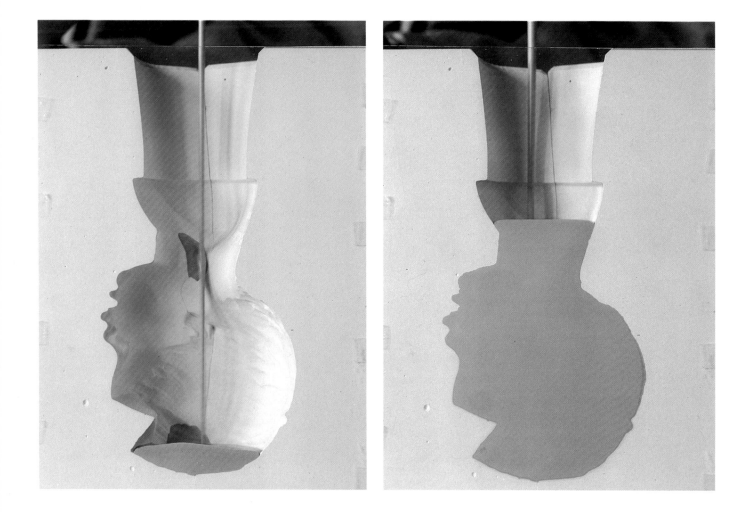

The plaster of paris mold absorbs water from the slip. At the proper time, the mold is turned over, enabling the water and excess slip to flow out. This leaves a hollow shell of moist ceramic, which forms the part.

All cast pieces are hollow as the result of this casting process. The cast head is shown in the bottom picture.

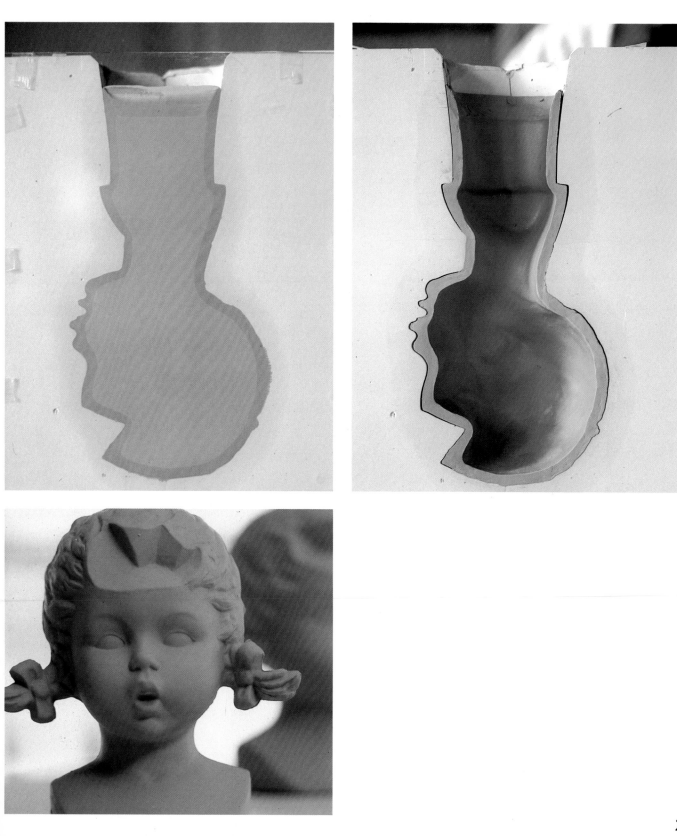

Left: Assembly of the figurine from its many pieces is a most delicate craft. Here, HUM 420, Is It Raining?, is being put together.

Above: Because the figurine is wet, it must be handled carefully. The umbrella is gently placed on HUM 152B, Umbrella Girl.

Overleaf: The assembler carefully places each piece, using the same liquid slip to adhere the parts. Here, a doll head is getting her front curls.

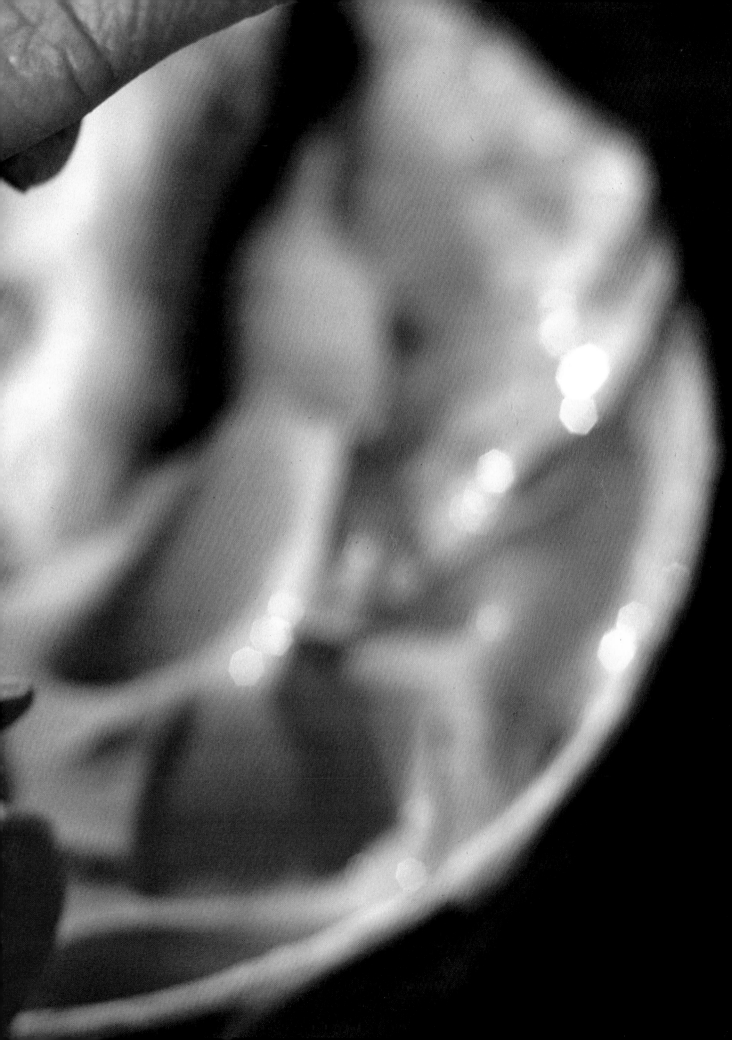

Above: The assembler's craft in-cludes detailing the nuances and fine points. These details, which may seem minor when observing the raw ceramic piece here, come to life with painting and firing.

Right: All pieces must be cleaned and all seams removed before the first firing.

Below: Tradition and high technology meet at the kiln. After the assembled figurine is dried at room temperature, it has its first (bisque) firing at about 2100 degrees (fahrenheit). Electricity is used for precise temperature control.

Right and overleaf: The glazing process, which follows the first firing, requires patience and a good eye. Hand-dipping reduces the possibility of chipping or breakage. The tint of the glaze ensures that the entire figurine receives the glaze.

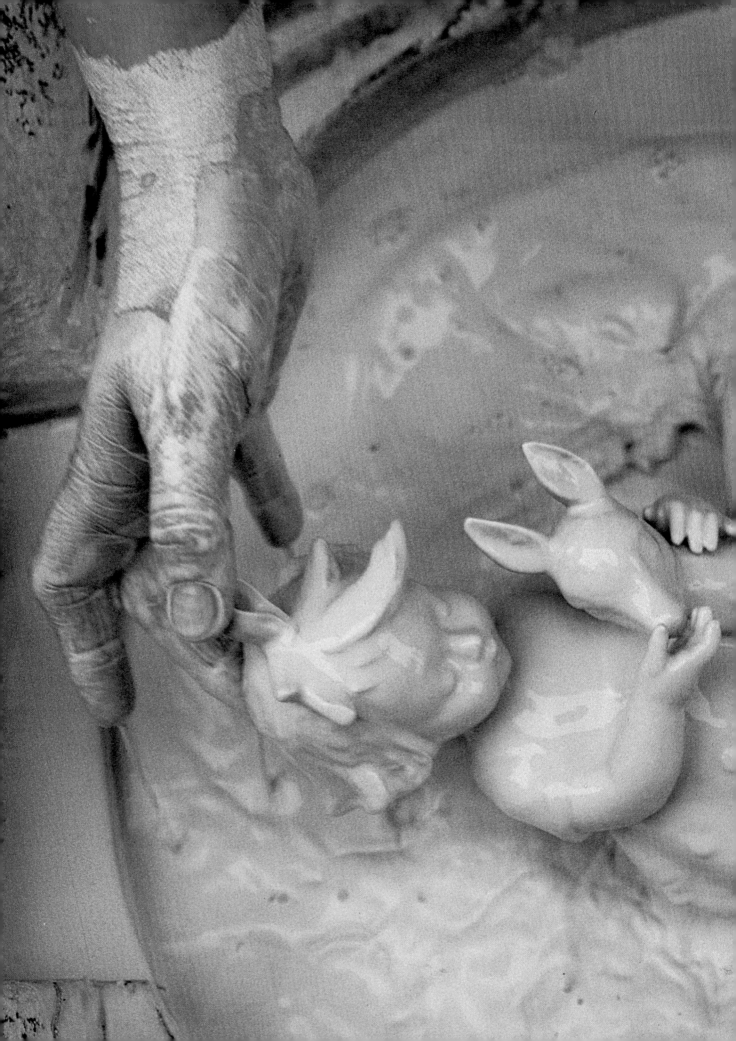

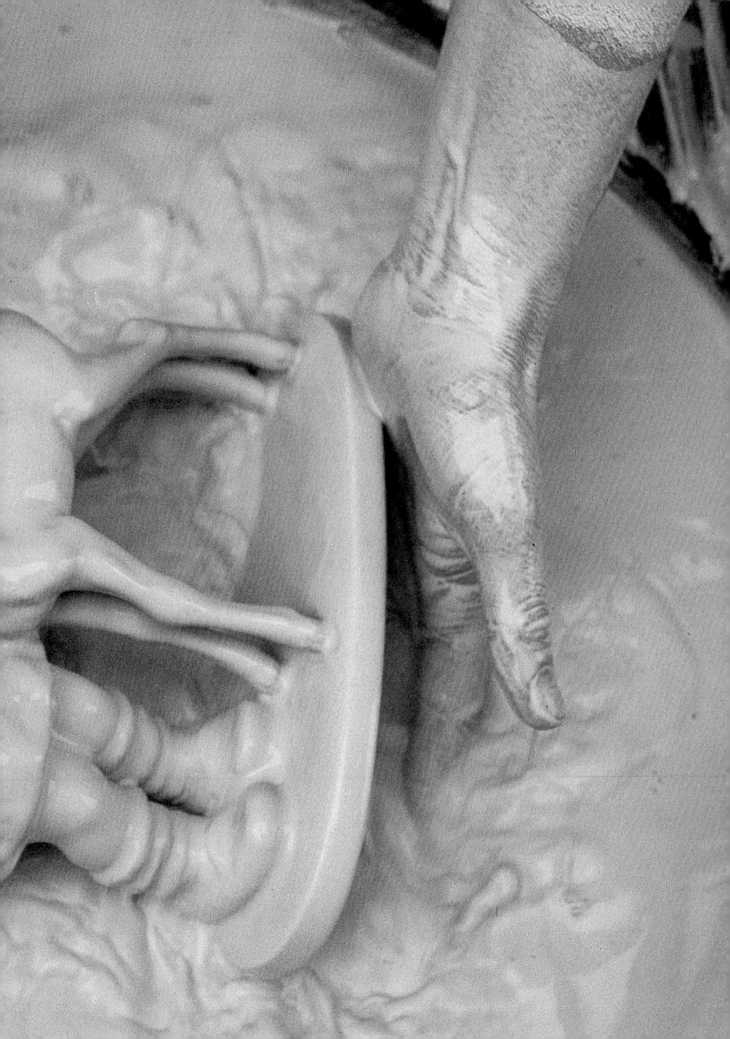

Left: When it emerges from the kiln after the second (glaze) firing, the figurine will be pure white.

Top: Richard Wahner, ovenmaster, charges and empties the big electric kilns. Waldemar Jahn, above left, and Stefan Kuhn, above right, are kiln department technicians. They make sure that their kilns are in top shape.

Overleaf: Chief Master Sample Painter Guenther Neubauer studies the colors of Sister Maria Innocentia Hummel's two-dimensional art. His selections will be painted on sample figurines, which will be taken to the Convent of Siessen for review and approval.

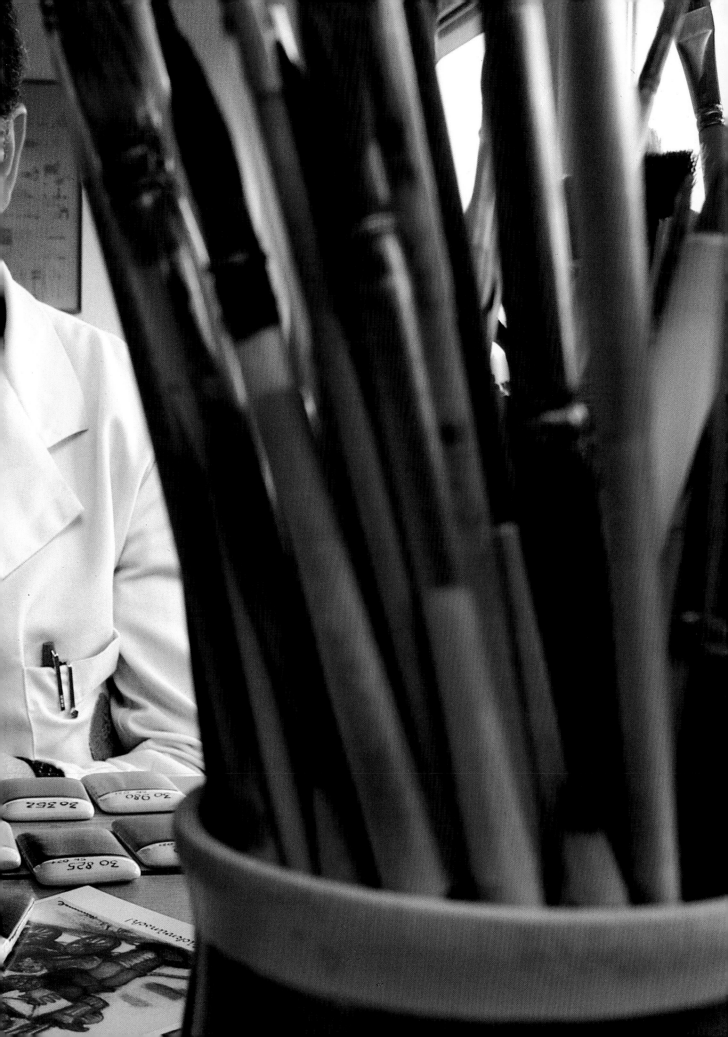

630	30 631	30 520	30 620	30 521	30 721	30 820	30 710	30 500	
+11	30 823	30 834	30 402	30 403	30 814	30 825	30 858	30 857	3
348	30 736	30 625	30 616	30 827	30 705	30 605	30 828	30 517	3
636	30 204	30 316	30 206	30 879	30 648	30 769	30 236	30 334	30
559	30 348	30 369	30 079	30 059	30 039	30 038	30 116	30 649	30
988	30 044	30 384	30 382	30 242	30 553	30 352	30 976	30 866	30
764	30 975	30 973	30 974	30 853	30 743	30 843	30 731	30 621	30
511	30 733	30 966	30 977	30 756	30 645	30 998	30 999	30 646	30
322	30 112	30 545	30 655	40 877	40 059	40 999	40 987	40 600	40

Left: A special color palette was created at the factory for M. I. Hummel figurines.

Above: Neubauer reviews the color samples to match as closely as possible the original art.

Overleaf: Metallic oxide paints in powder form, mixed with oil and a little turpentine, is a formula developed by the factory's ceramic paint chemists.

Above and right: Painting department supervisor Gunther Bauer mixes the ceramic paints. These are mixed under strict quality control, in small quantities, and are given out to painters only as needed.

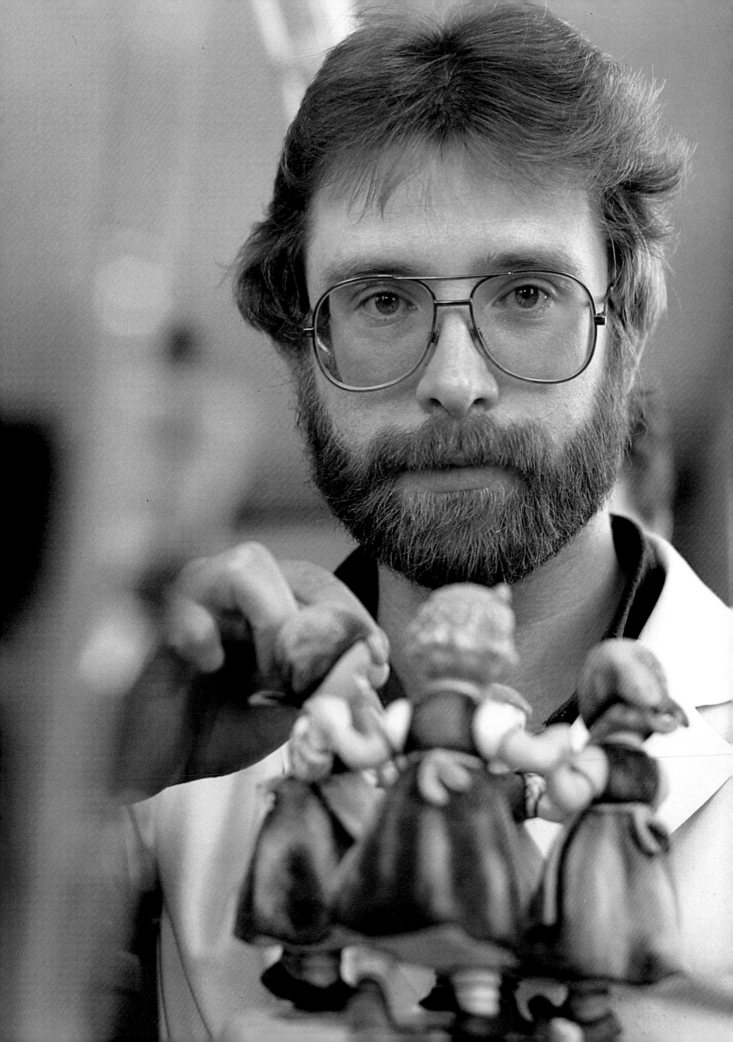

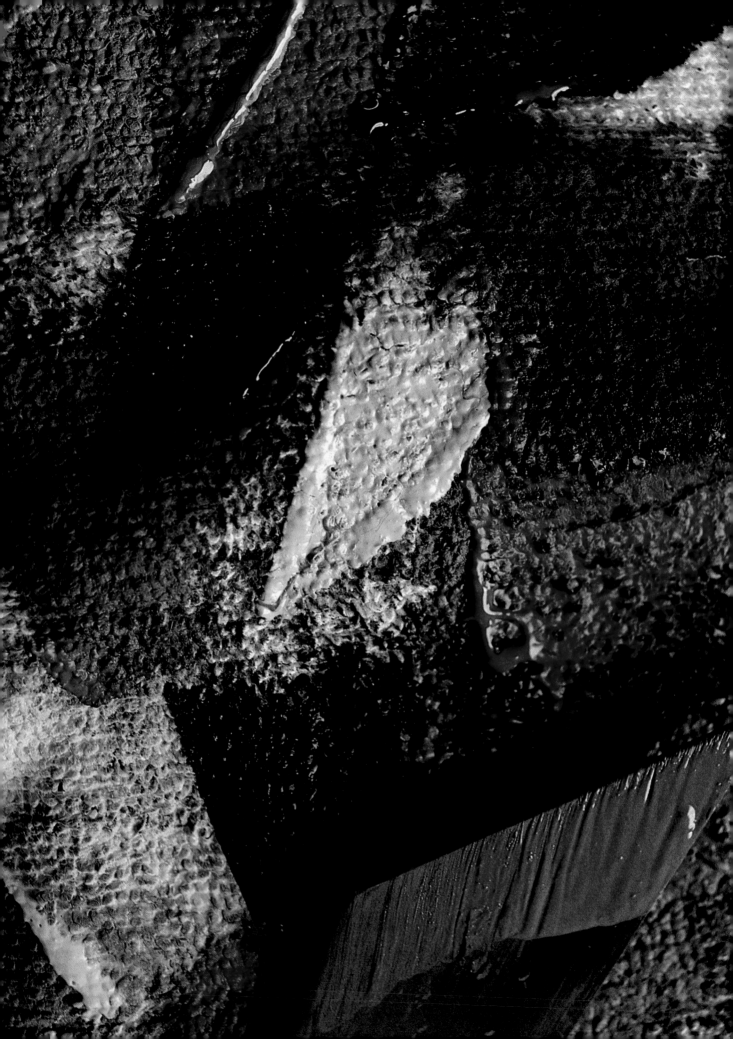

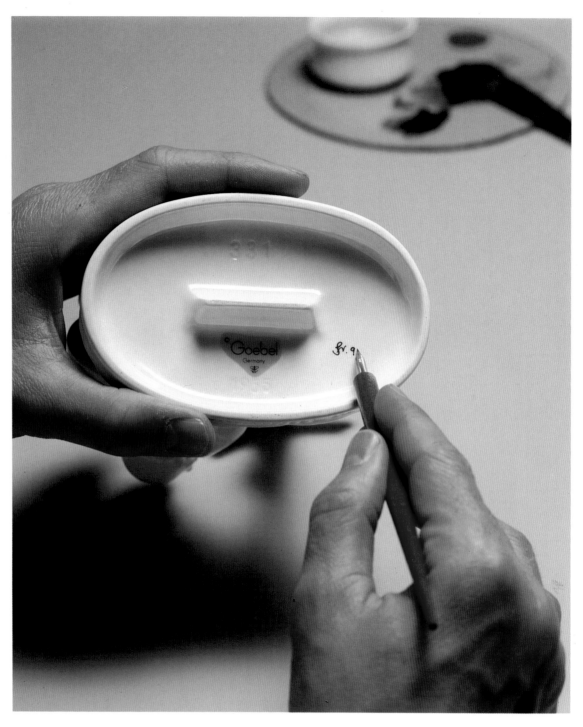

Left: *From bright colors come the figurines' soft hues.*

Above: *The identifying mark of a master painter is applied.*

Left: Edith Keilhammer paints a doll's head.

Top: Sharing knowledge is an ongoing tradition.

Above: The painting of a complete figurine is a painstaking task.

Above: Steffen Schmidt, left, creates sample pieces for casting. Bernd Schindhelm, right, is frequently seen executing his craft in the demonstration area for visitors at the factory.

Right: The love of the artisans for their work is reflected in the finished figurines.

Overleaf: Wolfgang Engel, a Goebel painter for more than a quarter of a century, helps bring HUM 348, Ring Around the Rosie, to life.

*Above: The hundreds of hand
operations involved in the creation of one figurine culminate
in the richness of the finished
treasure.*

*Right: Guenter Meyer, chief of
quality control, presides over
more than fifty quality check-
points, which are conducted
through every stage of production.*

*Overleaf: Master Sculptor Ger-
hard Skrobek works with the
young students. Goebel recruits
only the leading students from
Germany's technical high school
system and puts them through a
thorough three-year apprenticeship program.*

Left: Klaus Boehm is head of the Goebel painting school. His son is now carrying on the family tradition as an artisan at the factory.

Top: The students learn all phases of painting, just as they would at art school. Then they are sent to the Bavarian State School for Porcelain in Selb for technical training. As they mature, they will pass the Goebel tradition on to still another generation.

Above: Upon graduation from the apprenticeship program, students display the projects they have completed.

Overleaf: A montage of craftsmen's tools and components adds up to the completed work.

Second overleaf: The pastoral landscape belies the creative intensity within the factory.

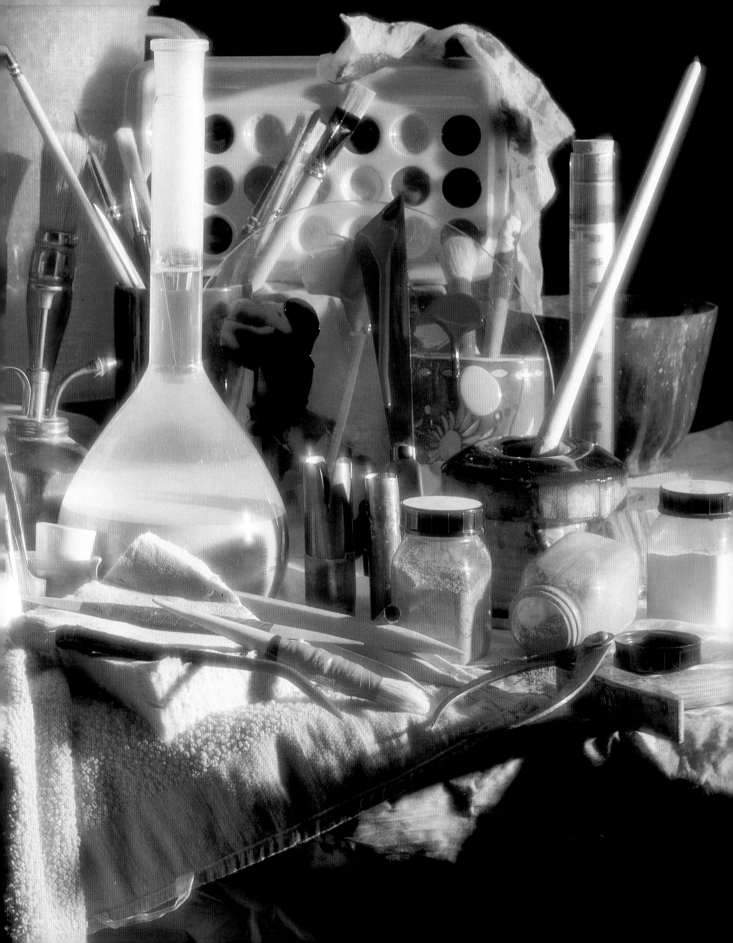

Hum	Bezeichnung / Modelleur	Internat. Musterschutz	Deutscher Musterschutz	Kloster Sießen
0345 X 1972	Der Kaufmann A Fair Measure (Skrobek) 5.6.72 Wählte 14.8.56 14 cm Stehender Junge als Kaufmann hinter Bank, mit Waage ob- wiegend, auf rundem Post.	18.7.57 4.12.72©	18.7.57 4.12.72	15.7.57 genehm.
Nr. Foto				
0346 1960	Das kluge Schwesterlein The smart little Sister Skrobek 22.10.56 11,5 cm Junge u. Mädchen auf Bank sitzend, Mädchen auf Schiefertafel schreibend auf Naturpostament	18.7.57 ©	18.7.57	15.7.57 genehmigt
Nr. 5902				
0347 1970	Die sieben Schwaben Aventure Bound, The seven Swabians Menzenbach 12.7.57 7 Jungen im Doppelreihe mit langem Spieß auf viereckigem Postament Größe 18,5 cm Post. 20,5 × 12 cm	8.10.57	8.10.57 ©	Ton Far ge
Nr. 14 239				
0348 1957	Ringelreihen Ring A round the Rosie Skrobek 27.8.57 Höhe 18 cm, Post.-Ø 16,5 cm 4 Mädchen tanzend und sich an d. Händen haltend, rundes Post.	31.10.57	31.10.57 ©	fertig geneh
Nr. 5619				
0349 1974	Der Blumenfreund The Florist Skrobek 1.11.57 18 cm stehender Junge, an Blume in der Hand riechend, davor Busch m. Blumen u. Vogel ovales Postament	18.4.61 ©	18.4.61 (1960)	lt. Schreiben v. 20.2. u. Vogel weglass genehmigt Arm u. Bl
Nr. 4774				
Postament				

Nr.	Bezeichnung / Modelleur	Internat. Mustersch.	Deutscher Mustersch.	Kloster Sießen	
350 980 5835	Zum Festtag On Holiday Skrobek 10.8.64 10,5 cm steh. Mädchen m. Korb u. Blumen a. l. Arm u. Regenschirm i. r. Hand. auf rundem Post.		9.9.65	Tonmodell am 23.10.64 genehmigt Farbiges Muster genehmigt am	MM ~~20~~ w ~~10~~ 6 6
351 982	Enzianfreude The Botanist Skrobek 14.4.65 11 cm Sitz. Mädchen m. Enzian- kranz u. 1 Blüte i. d. Händen, Vogel z. Rechten auf Naturpostament	1972	~~9.9.65~~ 29.5.72	Tonmodell genehmigt 21.7.65 Farbiges Muster genehmigt am	MM ~~22.6~~ ~~7~~ 6 7 2
352 980 974 5835	Ein süßer Gruß Sweet Greetings Skrobek 10.8.64 10,5 cm steh. Mädchen vor Zaun m. Lebkuchenherz auf ovalem Postament		9.9.65	Tonmodell am 23.10.64 genehmigt Farbiges Muster genehmigt am	MM ~~20~~ w ~~10~~ 6 6
353/0 353/I 1963 Größe I 619	15 ~~Frühlingstanz~~ 18 cm Frühlingstanz Skrobek 22.11.62 Spring Dance 2 Mädchen ohne Kopftuch von Hum 348 sich an den Händen fassend- tanzend ovales Post.	1963	1963 ©	genehmigt 20.5.63	MM KH
354 A 354 B 354 C	Weihkessel m. Engel " " " " " " von den später als Fig. genehmigt 357, 358, 359 moth. v. Unger ausgearb. v. Menzenbach	1961		} Vom Kloster abgelehnt am 15.9.65	

Below: Spring Cheer, HUM 72, *can chase away winter's doldrums*

Bottom: Apple Tree Boy, HUM 142, *may evoke memories of a collector's own children.*

The Realization of Dreams

M. I. Hummel figurines are a unique blend of human imagination and ceramic creation. They are the realization of the artistry and skill of many hands and minds, and the dreams and memories of countless others. They started their lives on the easel of one artist and continue through an intricate production process involving many others. But it is not until they are held close to the hearts of those who collect them that the dreams and memories begin to come to life.

> There was once a little girl who had a crush on a little boy. One day, as she was walking home from school, it suddenly began to rain. Without an umbrella, she was fast getting soaked. Out of nowhere an umbrella appeared, held over her head by the very object of her affections. Twenty years later, with a warm touch of nostalgia, *Stormy Weather* marked the start of her collection.

> A woman was poring over M. I. Hummel figurines on a store shelf, commenting to her friend as she progressed. Suddenly she spied *Apple Tree Boy* and cried, "Oh! Remember when Johnny was three and fell out of the tree? Doesn't this look just like him?" And another figurine entered an established collection.

> A student received her nursing diploma. *Little Nurse* was presented to her as a gift.

> Winter seemed to hang on forever. As an antidote, *Spring Cheer* was lovingly offered.

> After a particularly trying hospital stay, the joyous day of discharge came at last, and with it, the unexpected surprise of *Homeward Bound* to start the journey off right.

Memories of a beloved father are triggered by *Doctor*, or *Postman*, or *Little Tailor*; pre-concert jitters are soothed by *Little Fiddler*, or *Serenade*, or *Tuba Player*; new home owners are presented with that best of all good-luck omens, *Chimney Sweep* (whose German name translates into "I Bring Luck"). And so collectors are born. Some buy because memory is nudged by a specific motif. Others receive a gift to commemorate a special occasion or event. Still others "gift" themselves, because a face, an expression, a look, is totally irresistible.

"I'm Not a Collector"

There are those who protest: "I'm not a collector. I only buy what I like." According to Webster, buying what one likes fits the definition, for The Third New International (Unabridged) Edition states that a collection is: "A number of objects . . . that has been collected . . . according to some unifying principle or orderly arrangement."

The collector may well provide his or her own "unifying principle," for collecting of M. I. Hummel figurines is a distinctly personal pursuit. Just as there are no limits as to how many pieces make a collection, so there are no rules governing collecting itself. There are some who collect only figurines of boys, or of girls, because they have sons or daughters; some seek only double figurines (two figures on one base). It is not unusual for specific motifs, such as music-oriented figurines, to be the focal point of a collection, or for uniform height to be someone's personal requirement.

Just as often, however, the rationale (or "principle") for taking a figurine home is as simple as: "I couldn't resist it." That's the best reason of all, for one should collect only what one really loves. To select a figurine because one hopes that it will increase in value is to invite possible disappointment. While it's true that M. I. Hummel figurines have increased in value consistently over the years, predicting future secondary market values is a venture for the experts. If something does increase in value, that's a pleasant bonus. If it does not, and you have made your purchase because you loved the piece, your treasure will continue to be your treasure.

The Joys of Discovery

After the initial interest in M. I. Hummel figurines began in 1935, there was a temporary hiatus during the war years. When production resumed in 1946 (see Chapter I), American service personnel stationed in Germany discovered the figurines and spread the news by sending them as gifts to friends and relatives in the United States. As the world settled into new patterns in the 1950s, travel to Europe became popular for vacationing Americans, and commonplace for businessmen and women. A favorite stop for travelers was the Goebel factory in Roedental, still called Oeslau until the early 1970s. In those years it was possible for any visitors to the factory to have a tour behind the scenes and see the entire production process. Travel naturally included shopping for gifts, both for others and for oneself, and M. I. Hummel figurines, with their folkloric European look and their universal appeal, were a perfect choice. And the Hummel hunt was on!

Demand for the figurines soon became so great that, back in the United States, a shipment of figurines to a store would prompt the store owner to phone his list of customers, advising each that the specific figurine on request was at last in. It frequently happened that by the time all such calls had been made, there was nothing left to put on the shelves.

As happens with anything that is in such great demand, questions from both consumers and retailers began to flood the factory and the distributors in the United States: What is the meaning of this or

Below: Little Fiddler, HUM 2, *can calm pre-concert jitters.*

Bottom: Chimney Sweep, HUM 12, *is a good-luck omen for new home-owners.*

that mark on the base? Why does this figurine look different from that one, when it's the same motif? How should I clean my figurines? Where is the Hummel factory? It soon became apparent that a staff was needed just to handle such correspondence. And that's when the exciting, pacesetting and highly original decision was made—to start a club for Hummel enthusiasts.

The Club is Born

Preliminary planning, begun in 1975, focused on the needs of both collectors and retailers. Based on the premise that the more one knows about one's hobby, the more fun it can be, it was determined that the Club would be a collectors' information service. One of the first decisions was to develop a quarterly newsletter to answer questions and to keep members informed of new pieces as they were created. It was also determined that an M. I. Hummel figurine would be created each year that would be available only to Club members (and so marked, as part of its backstamp) and sold only through participating retailers. Each member would also receive a ceramic bisque plaque to serve as a "certificate" of membership.

The Goebel Collectors' Club, as it was then called, began operations in the spring of 1977. There was no way of knowing, in those early days, just how the public would respond to this totally new concept—no way of knowing that by the end of the first year, more than 100,000 members would proudly carry their membership cards.

And carry them they do. One favorite Club story is of the collector who, driving some distance on a dark, rainy night, suddenly realized the gas tank was nearing the empty mark. Gratefully spotting a small gas station, she pulled up. With a sinking feeling, she realized her funds were low, but she had credit cards as well as her checkbook. "No credit cards," said the proprietor, "and no checks, either." "But I have all this identification: see, my license, several credit cards . . ." "Hold on there," came the response. "Was that a membership card in that Goebel Club? That's okay, then. I'll take your check. My wife's a member."

The Club newsletter, originally, and briefly, called the *Goebel Collectors' Club News*, was renamed *INSIGHTS* and, in addition to the news and information originally included, also began carrying profiles of various artists, hints on how to display figurines, contests awarding M. I. Hummel prizes to the winners, insights into other collectors, and opportunities to learn more about the pieces. By the late 1980s, it had grown from the original six-page newsletter into a sixteen-page magazine.

Opposite page, left to right: I Brought You a Gift, HUM 479, *introduced in June 1989, is a g[ift] for new members of the M. I. Hummel Club. It was also a gi[ft] for those renewing their mem-bership in 1989–90.* Two Hands[,] One Treat, HUM 493, *was the [ ] renewal gift in 1991–92.*

Below: The plaque, Smiling Through, HUM 690, *was the s[ec]-ond exclusive collectible for members of the Goebel Colle[c]-tors' Club (now the M. I. Hum-mel Club), offered in 1978–79.*

Top: Honey Lover, HUM 312, was introduced in 1991 exclusively for fifteen-year members of the M. I. Hummel Club.

Above: The Little Pair, HUM 449, is an exclusive offering for ten-year members of the M. I. Hummel Club.

Opposite page, left to right: Flower Girl, HUM 548, is available only to five-year members of the M. I. Hummel Club, while Gift from a Friend, HUM 485, is the exclusive Club offer for 1991–92.

Above: Each plate in the Celebration Series, now closed editions, was offered to members of the Club for one year only, Top, left to right: Valentine Joy, HUM 737 (1987–88); It's Cold, HUM 735 (1989–90). *Bottom, left to right:* Daisies Don't Tell, HUM 736 (1988–89); Valentine Gift, HUM 738 (1986–87).

Local Chapters Organized

The concept of Local Club Chapters began in 1978, as members began organizing themselves with enthusiasm. As the years went on, Local Chapter meetings developed into learning sessions, exploring such points of constant fascination as: comparison of the original art of Sister Maria Innocentia to the finished figurine; comparison of several models of the same motif to note variations; display techniques, such as combining figurines with flowers; slide presentations showing Club tours or in-store artist appearances; demonstrations of how a black light can often be used to detect repairs to a figurine, and much more. Chapter meetings led to greater knowledge, and to expanded friendships among collectors.

The first of five annual National Local Chapter Conventions took place in 1981. By 1986, the National Convention was being held every other year, and Inter-Chapter Conferences were introduced. These take members all over North America, as individual Chapters play host in their own home towns to members from other Chapters. Attendees travel far and wide to participate, networking and enjoying the camaraderie that has become an informal benefit of Club membership.

Roedental—The Collector's Mecca

The factory has remained a magnet, drawing visitors constantly. In 1985, in celebration of fifty years of M. I. Hummel figurines, the Club initiated a travel program which offers members several trips each year. The itineraries are varied, and have included Italy, Hungary, Switzerland, Austria, Holland and France. Always on the agenda are glorious days spent at the Convent of Siessen, where the sisters' greeting is open and warm, and that "Mecca" for collectors, the factory in Roedental.

The travelers are taken on a special tour through the factory itself, and treated to an in-depth look at the production of their favorite collectibles. (It is only on these trips that this production tour is presented.) The delight in traveling with others who share one's hobby enhances the pleasure of members who participate in the travel program; many do so more than once.

Below: The Sisters at the Convent of Siessen love to greet visitors.

Bottom: Travelers on a Club trip gathered for a photo at a formal reception in Coburg.

Below: The six-foot Merry Wanderer welcomes visitors to the factory in Roedental in a very special way. Here two Club members pose with the well-known figure.

The thirst for knowledge among Club members has fostered many programs within programs. Seminars conducted by Club personnel can spring up at the drop of a question, and this happens often on Club trips. Seminars have also become a feature during the major collector shows each year, most notably at the International Collectible Exposition in South Bend, Indiana, held each July.

Collections Add to Home Decor

Many collectors display their figurines behind glass doors enjoying the splash of color and the various groupings they create. Others feel that the figurines should make a statement about themselves and their interests, and so like to use them in room decor, placing figurines such as *Book Worm* or *Thoughtful* on or near bookshelves, and *Hello* on a desk, near a telephone. Figurines with garden or outdoor motifs are often seen next to, or nestled in, a plant or bouquet of flowers. The Club has developed programs that encourage collectors to think of their figurines as part of home decor. Articles in *INSIGHTS* illustrate this theme, and the Club sponsors decorating contests at the various collector shows, too.

The Club Becomes International

By 1989, it was clear that the fascination with collecting was growing in other parts of the world. Several countries in Europe were showing an upswing in sales, and the Far East, particularly Japan, had begun to show major interest. The time was right for expansion, and on June 1, 1989, the International M. I. Hummel Club was born. European activity began in Germany, Austria and Switzerland, soon followed by The Netherlands, Belgium, Sweden and Great Britain. Today, the International M. I. Hummel Club has members from thirty nations.

There were changes in the new-member package as well. The bisque plaque gave way to *I Brought You A Gift*, an M. I. Hummel figurine that commemorates one's entry into the Club. The binder, which all members had received since the start of the Club for holding their copies of *INSIGHTS*, was redesigned and pages of valuable information added. Renewal gifts, presented to members when they rejoin for another year, may include an M. I. Hummel figurine, jewelry or other Hummel-related treasures.

Look-Alikes Enchant

The M. I. Hummel Figurine Look-Alike Contest is one activity that collectors in the United States have adopted wholeheartedly. Begun by the company many years ago, it was conducted as a photographic contest until 1985. In 1977, during the first Hummel Festival held in Eaton, Ohio, a live look-alike contest was also inaugurated, which continues today around the country, frequently

Top: One lucky winner of an
M. I. Hummel Figurine Look-
Alike Contest held in South
Bend, Indiana, represented Little
Fiddler.

Above: A group of M. I. Hummel Figurine Look-Alike contes-
tants line up for a curtain call in
South Bend.

Two new backstamps of special interest to collectors made their debuts in 1991. Written in German and English, they mark both introduction and retirement of a figurine. Shown here are the bases of (left), Grandma's Girl, HUM 561 (also showing the new M. I. Hummel backstamp; see page 304), and Globe Trotter, HUM 79. As of January 1991, first and final issues are also indicated on special tags, as well as backstamps, as seen at right on Globe Trotter.

The special backstamp for the Century Collection figurine, Let's Tell the World, HUM 487, signifies fifty-five years of production of M. I. Hummel figurines.

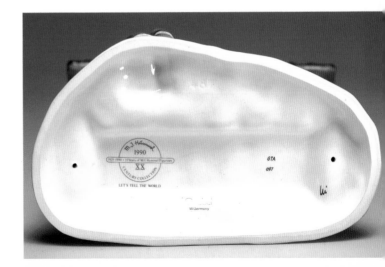

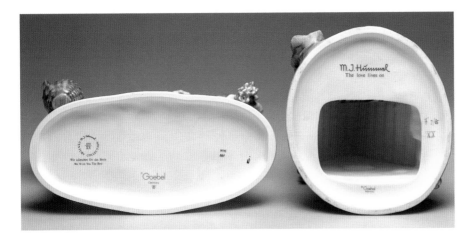

The evolution of the markings on the bases for the Century Collection, with XX signifying twentieth century, is illustrated here. At left we see the mark as it now appears on We Wish You the Best, HUM 600 *(1991); at right we see it handwritten by an artist for the first-year release on* Chapel Time, HUM 442 *(1986).*

The base of Supreme Protection, HUM 364 *(left), shows the unique backstamp for this closed edition. The base of* Jubilee, HUM 416, *shows the backstamp for this figurine which commemorates fifty years of production of M. I. Hummel figurines.*

The backstamps for numbered limited editions commemorate special events, such as Crossroads, HUM 331 *(left) and* Land in Sight, HUM 530. *(See Chapter 2 for more on these two figurines.)*

These two figurines were designed in 1954 by Master Sculptor Arthur Moeller, Angel Duo on Tree (praying and harp), HUM 236A, and Angel Duo on Tree (trumpet and mandolin), 236B, are both closed numbers.

Happy Pastime, HUM 221, is a candy box with a closed number. This piece was never released.

Madonna, HUM 222, a plaque in a metal frame (left), is a closed edition; Madonna & Child, HUM 249, an unframed plaque, was a sample only which was never produced, and is a closed number.

Left to right: HUM 205 is a German plaque for M. I. Hummel dealers; it is now a closed edition. HUM 460, an M. I. Hummel authorized retailer's plaque called The Tally, was produced in several languages (Dutch, German, Italian, French, Swedish and Spanish) for international use. The American version is a closed edition. HUM 187A is an M. I. Hummel Authorized Retailer's Plaque featuring The Merry Wanderer, which was reintroduced in 1990 and is currently available to participating retailers.

sponsored by individual stores. Children in full costume, with detailed props, are called onstage to pose for judges who evaluate them (with great difficulty!) as to their resemblance to the figurine they represent. Prizes are awarded, and the happy winners go home with more figurines for their collections.

The Rare and the Unusual

As collectors grow more knowledgeable over the years, rare and unusual figurines come to the surface. For example, in 1976, noted collector Robert L. Miller came into the possession of eight M. I. Hummel figurines in Hungarian dress. Since then, twenty-four prototypes have been discovered, showing figurines in the clothing of children of Bulgaria, Serbia, Sweden, Czechoslovakia and Hungary. Although records at the factory from the late 1930s are not complete, it seems that there were plans to produce M. I. Hummel figurines in "international" dress, based on drawings done by Sister Maria Innocentia. With the escalation of the war, however, the plans were abandoned and the figurines were never produced. The pieces that surfaced are production samples.

A number of figurines have been remodeled over the years. There can be many reasons for remodeling; as mentioned in Chapter I, when production resumed in 1946 the original molds for some pieces had been lost or destroyed. In other cases, the demands of the production process necessitated new designs. For example, some elements of certain figurines were simply too fragile to be produced and had to be redesigned.

Individual Creativity Plays a Part

Although each figurine must adhere to the original intent of the two-dimensional art of Sister Maria Innocentia, it's important to remember that the work at the factory is done by individual artists, not machines. Therefore it is likely that, upon close scrutiny of two samples of the same motif, one might be able to detect some differences. For example, it is not unusual for a painter to look at a number of figurines on the shelf at a store and single one out, saying: "I did that one." Not every decorator uses the same technique in a brush stroke and, to the educated eye, these subtleties are visible.

More readily visible are differences in the look of the sculpting of a piece. It is not difficult to see the differences between a figurine sculpted by either of the two early masters, Reinhold Unger and Arthur Moeller, and one sculpted by the later master, Gerhard Skrobek. Skrobek developed a more textural finish, to his mind representative of the folkloric art of Sister Maria Innocentia.

The Challenges of Translation

What is meant when we speak of translating the original art into the three-dimensional figurine? Can it be a direct translation, with

Overleaf, left to right: In the late 1980s the coloring of With Loving Greetings, HUM 309, *was changed; the inkpot went from blue to brown and the message went from deep turquoise to periwinkle blue. The coloring on* Sensitive Hunter, HUM 6, *was changed in the early 1980s when the rabbit was made brown rather than the original orange.*

no changes at all? How is the third dimension—that part that is not visible, but only suggested, on the original art—decided upon and added? These are the sculptor's challenges. He or she must retain the feel of the original two-dimensional art, while making it appear totally natural in ceramic. In addition, the sculptor must determine how best to convey the mood and original intent when there are some elements in the original that clearly would not work in a sculpture. For example, a bird flying overhead in a picture could not become part of a simple rendering of a child in three dimensions. Should it be included elsewhere? Perhaps on a gate, or a tree, or even the child's shoe? Or should it be eliminated entirely?

These are questions that must be addressed by the creative team before any figurine is approved. The all-important criterion of carrying out the intent of the original artist must be upheld. Meeting this challenge is one of the triumphs of the collaboration among all the artists involved.

Opening Up One's World

To the uninitiated, collecting is the gathering of inanimate objects. To those in the know, collecting is the opening up of a new world. It is an opportunity to expand one's knowledge of history, to explore various elements of art, to gain insight into oneself, and to broaden one's circle of friends.

In actively collecting M. I. Hummel figurines, enthusiasts open up their world in all these ways. By looking into the backgrounds of Sister Maria Innocentia Hummel and the Goebel company, and learning how these two entities came together, the collector can delve into the social and economic conditions of that era. To examine the adaptation of two-dimensional art into three-dimensions is to look at an important aspect of art. In studying the school of art that had the greatest influence on Sister Maria Innocentia we learn a great deal about the *Deutsche Werkbund,* which took as its base the traditions of the Baroque and Florentine periods. Even exploring ways to make a collection part of home decor is to bring an artistic study into one's home.

Personal, and family, insights are gained as collectors suddenly discover a common thread running through a seemingly unfocused collection. Cross-country friendships are cultivated among Club members, while members of Local Chapters have the ongoing opportunity to meet new people with whom they can share ideas. And Club members are looking forward to developing a network on an international scale in the years to come.

More than one collector has been heard to say: "These are my children." M. I. Hummel figurines are held close to their hearts, for they are more than inanimate objects. Through everything they signify, they have come to mean life, in all its forms and expressions.

Comparing the original artwork of Sister Maria Innocentia Hummel, top, to a completed figurine such as Photographer, HUM 178, above, allows the collector to truly appreciate the talent and skill of all those involved in translating the two-dimensional art into the beloved three-dimensional collectibles.

REMEMBERING SISTER MARIA INNOCENTIA HUMMEL
AND HER ROLE IN GERMAN FOLKLORIC ART

The Tradition of Children in Art

To appreciate the importance of Sister Maria Innocentia's work and to understand her place in the history of art, we need to look back to earlier times and consider the traditional representations of children in art.

Since antiquity, the child has been a favorite subject, always idealized as a symbol of innocence. For centuries Western art was preoccupied with religion, and the child, in this context, was encountered either in the form of the baby Jesus or, after the European Renaissance of the fifteenth and sixteenth centuries, as a cherub or angel, still representing innocence, goodness and purity. Not until the middle of the eighteenth century, when the writings of the French philosopher Jean-Jacques Rousseau were published, did the child begin to be seen as an individual. Rousseau wrote that mankind would only be saved when it returned to *l'état naturel*—to the natural and simple form of life as it is lived in the innocent and serene countryside. Rousseau's ideal human being was the unspoiled child, still capable of being educated to be a "natural human being." Rousseau's philosophy strongly influenced many of the great thinkers, writers and artists of his time.

In 1710, the first European porcelain factory was founded at Meissen in Germany. During the time of Rousseau, Meissen and Sèvres in France, founded forty-six years later, were the most important manufactories of the century and created a wealth of figurines representing myths and legends from ancient Greece and Rome, characters from the Commedia dell'Arte (stock Italian comedies of the sixteenth to eighteenth centuries), courtspeople and craftsmen. Often the porcelain pieces were based upon two-dimensional etchings by famous artists. It is mainly in these early porcelain figurines that we first see three-dimensional representations of children outside of a religious context. These eighteenth-century pieces are the true ancestors of M. I. Hummel figurines, and the roots from which these contemporary collectibles have grown.

Berta Hummel: An Early Talent

Sister Maria Innocentia Hummel was born Berta Hummel on May 21, 1909, in the rural Bavarian village of Massing an der Rott. The third of six children born to merchant Adolf Hummel and his wife Viktoria, Berta was artistically inclined and gifted from a very early age. As a young child she scribbled her impressions on the blank corners of newspapers. When her father was away from home, she would illustrate her letters to him. Once a schoolgirl, she happily rendered friendly caricatures and quick portraits of classmates. Often came the cry, "Sketch me, Berta Hummel!"

Opposite page: This self-portrait by the artist was done before she entered the Convent of Siessen.

Below: "Girl with Birdcage" is a porcelain figurine from 1753 by Blondeau after an etching by Boucher. It was produced by the French factory Vincennes, which became Sèvres in 1756. (Photo courtesy of Musée du Louvre, Paris, France) c photo R.M.N.

Bottom: This four-inch-high replica in the Little Bavaria *series represents Sister Maria Innocentia's birthplace.*

Preceding page: This photo features the parish church of St. Markus at the Convent of Siessen. The open window in the adjoining building to the right of the church marks Sister Maria Innocentia Hummel's atelier. A four-inch high reproduction of this church is one of the pieces represented in the Little Bavaria *series.*

Her father, who himself had artistic aspirations, but who had been obliged to enter the family business rather than pursue an artistic career, was pleased with his daughter's talent and encouraged her. During Berta's early schooling at the local Catholic school in Massing, her unmistakable artistic gift was also encouraged by one of her later teachers, who recommended her for admission to the Marienhoehe, a boarding school run by the English Sisters, at Simbach am Inn, about twenty miles east of Massing. At Marienhoehe, Berta received a traditional secondary-school education and developed her instinctive skills through training in watercolor and pen and pencil sketches. Her research into forms and schools of art must have been intensive for, at the age of 16, while still at Marienhoehe, she accomplished a landscape revealing knowledge beyond her formal studies. Again, one of her teachers took a special interest in her talent and became her mentor, advising her to apply to the Munich Academy of Applied Arts.

Berta was accepted and, in the fall of 1927, at eighteen, the young artist began her studies in Munich with the renowned professors Max Dasio, Else Brauneis and F. Wirnhier. The director of the academy at the time was Carl Sattler, an important representative of the Werkbund movement, which was attempting to create a fusion between the tradition of religious art and contemporary design. At the academy Berta became immersed in anatomy classes, oil painting and watercolor. She executed many exceptional works during this period, including some expressionistic flower and fruit still lifes. While at the academy Berta Hummel also did some of her best portrait studies, as well as two self-portraits, including the one in pencil seen on page 284.

Art and Religion: A Bavarian Tradition

Looking back at Berta Hummel's early artistic gift and her rigorous, traditional training in the best schools of her time, it is no surprise that she became a well-known artist. Her direction was clear from childhood. Her decision to become a Franciscan Sister was, in a way, the surprise, for nothing in her earlier life pointed her towards that path. And yet it is important to remember the age-old linkage of religion and art, which was especially strong in the deeply religious, tradition-bound land of Bavaria. The example of the sisters who were her early artistic mentors, the friendship with two Franciscan Sisters at the academy and the influence of the art she studied and executed, came together in her decision to enter the Franciscan Convent of Siessen. She did so in April 1931, following her graduation from the Munich Academy and completion of the first state examination for the teaching of art in secondary schools. Eventually, in August 1934, she took her vows at Siessen.

While at the convent, as a candidate, Berta Hummel taught art at the secondary school for girls, St. Anna, in the nearby town of Saulgau/Wuerttemberg. It became a custom among the families in Saulgau to have their children's portraits painted by her; some of

Above: Berta Hummel was seventeen when she was graduated from the Institute of English Sisters at Marienhoehe. Right: As a student at the Munich Academy of Applied Arts, she posed with her teachers and other students for this photo. Berta is standing, second from the left, in the foreground (in v-necked shirt). Sister M. Laura Brugger is in the front row, to her right is Professor Else Brauneis, and in the middle of the back row is Professor Maximilian Dasio. Above Right: On June 4, 1933, she bade her family farewell to join the Convent at Siessen. Berta is at left, her parents Viktoria and Adolf Hummel are sitting, and to Berta's right are: her sister Centa, brother Franz, sister and brother-in-law Katharina and Georg Edenhofer and brother Adolf Hummel. (Photos courtesy of Alfred Hummel)

While still a student, Berta Hummel painted this oil-on-canvas landscape of Massing an der Rott, with its parish church featured prominently.

Right: The Massing church is also represented in the ceramic Little Bavaria series. It is approximately four inches high.

Sister Maria Innocentia's drawing, Annunciation of Mary, *demonstrates how she held to a tradition of religious art that developed over centuries of European cultural history.*

whom later became local notables. In the convent itself, much of her artistic responsibility lay in the design of clerical vestments and altar cloths, subsequently embroidered by other sisters. This work done at Siessen was well known in South Africa, in the United States and in Brazil. After taking her vows she was promoted to the head of that department, and introduced a new, more modern style that did not sacrifice the impressive embroideries for which the Convent was known.

In her atelier, Sister Maria Innocentia designed and executed a number of fine altar paintings in oil on canvas. Her works also included images of saints and the Madonna and Child. She used a variety of techniques: pastels, oil on canvas and pastel combined with gouache and tempera. The latter was possibly her preferred technique. Thin Outline sketches for watercolors were left as a decorative element. The Fourteen Stations of the Cross, a sequence of breathtaking studies that could be considered her most personal and demanding work, were executed in pure watercolors.

It was in the seclusion of the Convent of Siessen that she accomplished the work that would make her name known throughout the world. Drawing with charcoal and pastel on sheets of mill-finished drawing paper, she brought to life the M. I. Hummel children. Sometimes she also rendered these in small formats, on canvas, using oil or watercolor. While most of the subjects we know today are cheerful and endearing ones, her motifs were not always merry. Sister Maria Innocentia lived in a stressful era, and sometimes her drawings and paintings reflected the social problems of her time.

The Beginning of Critical Acclaim

While she was still a postulant, the young artist had been invited to display her work at the annual exhibitions accompanying the celebrations at the profession and at the *Künstlertage* (artist's days) at the convent of Beuron. Her art had come to the attention of religious art publishers, several of whom began publishing her religious illustrations as well as other motifs featuring children in the form of fine art prints. Beginning in 1932 her art was also seen in exhibitions at Saulgau and Stuttgart (at the *Wuerttembergischer Kunstverein*). In 1933, an exhibition was held at the Convent of Siessen, and among the visitors was the art critic of the *Saulgauer Nationalzeitung*, who was greatly impressed by what he saw. A translation of his article about the exhibit reads:

The reviewer visited the Franciscan Convent of Siessen in the early morning of a beautiful day. He was even happier to go there as he had learnt that the works of a very special, divinely gifted artist were to be given special attention. This artist is Berta Hummel, Sister Maria Innocentia by her Convent name. She had become known in the town of Saulgau by some paintings shown in a shop window there.

Already at the door the eye is caught by a painting that shows Jesus Christ crucified. Though only the result of intuition, the refined technique reveals the artist's considerable ability to fix the mood of a passing moment.

She was already starting to gain recognition as an important artist in 1933, when she completed Saint Francis, *top,* and Mary, Queen of May, *above.*

Opposite page: Loving Mother and Child *is one of Sister Maria Innocentia's more colorful religious works.*

Then the scope widens and the eye becomes aware of the most delightful and original paintings of children this young artist is able to produce: it is a very special charm which captures the viewer's attention and causes his thoughts to return to the fairyland of his childhood. These characters drawn so vividly and impulsively, so warmly and compassionately in all clarity, reveal the artist's ability to look deeply into a child's heart and to express distinctively what travels like a golden thread through all the years of childhood.

If we were not already convinced that children were, from the beginning, the dominating subject of her artwork, the preceding text would certainly persuade us that this was the case. And, given her vocation, we might add that she portrayed both earthly and heavenly children, rendering them from those she saw around her as well as from memories of her own youth. They could have been reflections of her own self, too. Her work may have been an attempt to master the complexities of the world via brush and pencil. And perhaps, when she took pencil to paper, she could hear a voice whisper in her ear: "Sketch me, Berta Hummel!"

In 1934, the Emil Fink Verlag in Stuttgart published art prints, art cards and an art book depicting Sister Maria Innocentia Hummel's works blended with poems specifically written by the poetess Margarete Seemann to match the pictures. It was entitled *Das Hummel Buch* (The Hummelbook) and was an immediate success.

The Convent also allowed a Munich-based publisher to publish and distribute Hummel art cards on a variety of subjects throughout Europe.

A Fulfilling Religious and Artistic Career

The discovery of Sister Maria Innocentia's work by Franz Goebel and the subsequent successful production of the M. I. Hummel figurines in the second half of the 1930's marked a rich era for the young sister. She lived a contemplative life within her religious order, including teaching, working with children and painting. These were prolific and happy years for Sister Maria Innocentia, in which she fulfilled her natural talents as an artist and a sister.

Her relationship with Goebel during that time is worth considering as another happy and natural fusion of two rich traditions: that of a successful portraitist of children meeting that of an established figurine maker, both of them steeped in the history and aura of the region. Her collaboration with Goebel is a harkening back to the eighteenth-century figurines of Meissen based upon prints by famous artists of that time. The Goebel family originally came from the village of Wallendorf, thirty-five miles from Oeslau, and known as the cradle of the Thuringian porcelain industry. Fifty years after Meissen's founding, alchemists in Wallendorf had independently discovered the formula for making porcelain, and many flourishing factories were built in this area. Goebel's production began with dinnerware and other useful items, but by 1890

figurines were already a large part of their line, including a wide range of children with both classical and contemporary motifs. When Max Louis Goebel, the founder's grandson, took over in 1911, he began the custom of collaborating with well-known artists of the time. And when his son, Franz Goebel, asked Sister Maria Innocentia to allow his company to produce her children's pictures in three dimensions, he was following the time-honored tradition established before him, not only by his forebears, but also by figurine makers of the past two hundred years.

The Difficult Years

In 1935, when she began her advanced studies in Munich the happy era of Sister Maria Innocentia's life began to take on forebodings of the hardships to come. Her own health began to falter; respiratory problems forced her to rest for extended periods of time, either at the convent or in nearby sanatoriums. Negative critical commentaries of her work appeared in Nazi publications. None of these problems stopped her from working.

In November 1940 the German government turned the Convent into a repatriation center for ethnic Germans who had formerly resided in countries that were now occupied by the German army. The sisters at the convent of Siessen were sent home to their families; Sister Maria Innocentia was among them, but she was allowed to return after a few weeks. Living conditions at the convent were not good; the residents were permanently short of heating, food and medical supplies. Artists' materials were, of course, far down on the list of priorities. Printing paper was in such short supply that it was available for export only, and Sister Maria Innocentia was even unable to obtain one of her own printed drawings. After 1940, the life of a sister and artist, even one in good health, was filled with hardships. For Sister Maria Innocentia, whose repiratory problems grew, by 1944, into pleurisy, pain and suffering were daily companions.

And yet, even during these most difficult times, she continued to paint and draw and to serve as an inspiration to others. It is interesting to see that in her early years as an artist she painted those of her works that show children in distress or helping the distressed, while in later years, which brought so much hardship to herself and her surroundings, she created her pictures of merry children.

In spite of conditions of extreme deprivation for both her health and her spiritual and artistic needs, the early 1940's were another extraordinarily prolific era for Sister Maria Innocentia, perhaps more so than any other. Though slowed by weakness and interrupted by prolonged stays in sanatoriums, her creative impulse always returned. She continued her successful artistic work until her untimely death on November 6, 1946.

Above: Slumber Time *was drawn in November, 1940, after the Siessen Convent was turned into a camp for repatriated Germans.*

Opposite page: The four themes of the cards shown here are the basis for several M. I. Hummel figurines. These drawings were done in the late 1930s, at the end of her most prolific period. Clockwise from top left: Little Scholar, Little Tailor, Latest News and Postman.

Sister Maria Innocentia's Mainz Madonna and Child is a classic example of the religious art tradition during the first half of the twentieth century. Often overlooked, her religious art helps set a classical standard of this genre for our time.

A Child of Her Time

Sister Maria Innocentia's portrayals of children reflect her deep roots in the religious Bavarian countryside of her childhood, her thorough artistic studies and her keen sense of the time in which she lived. Like the children often featured in art, hers are both a reminder of childhood paradise and hope for a better future. The innocent imitation of adult activities is a favorite theme for portrayals of children, and certainly many of Sister Maria Innocentia's figures fall into this category. But some of the craftspeople and tradespeople she created were actually based on real people she knew. Often, too, some of the children she drew represented the social ills she saw around her, but for political reasons, the names she gave these pieces, such as "Begging Children" or "For the Hungry" had to be changed to more complacent ones, such as "Going to Grandma's." Her musicians are perhaps the creations most rooted in her folkloric traditions. One art critic wrote, in 1933: "We feel that she only draws from one source, the inexhaustible fount of our folklore which should be sacred to us, and which causes us to write about such artist's work. The pictures radiate the German *Gemüt*, which we encounter in the works of Ludwig Richter without imitating him. Each one of her paintings is original and new, has its own charm which is even increased by an elegant, not to say musical composition."

The universal and timeless appeal of Sister Maria Innocentia's art lives on in many dimensions today. The spirit of this religious and artistic woman is captured by the Hummel images that are both classic and timely for our age, as they were for hers. They will certainly continue to bring inspiration and love into the hearts of all who glimpse them in years to come.

Opposite page: Sister Maria Innocentia's classical training and studies of the Old Masters are evident in her Mother of God.

Overleaf: Sister Maria Innocentia's triptych, oil on canvas, Altar Picture, *was done during the 1930s.*

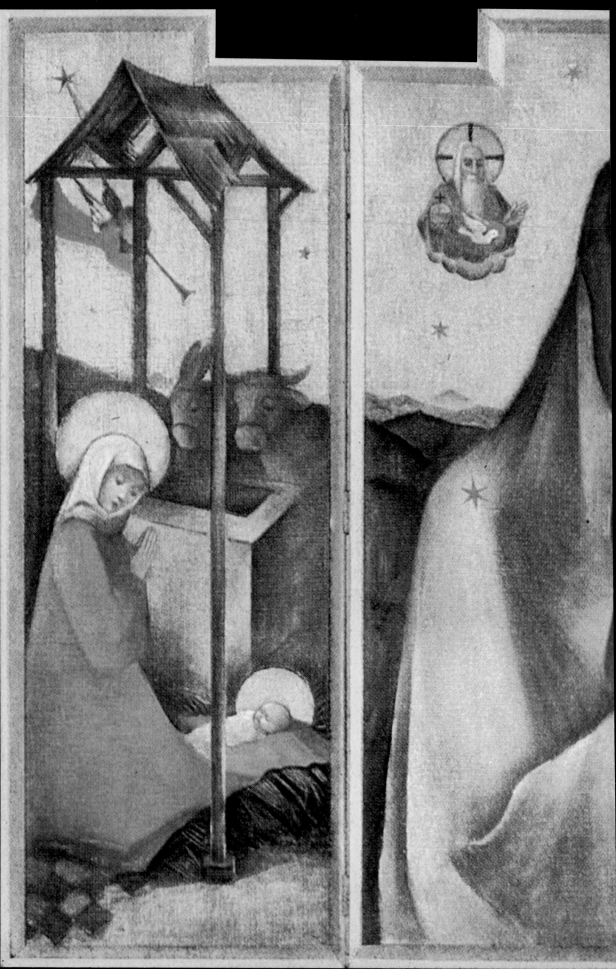

APPENDIX: A HISTORY OF THE MARKS AND SYMBOLS

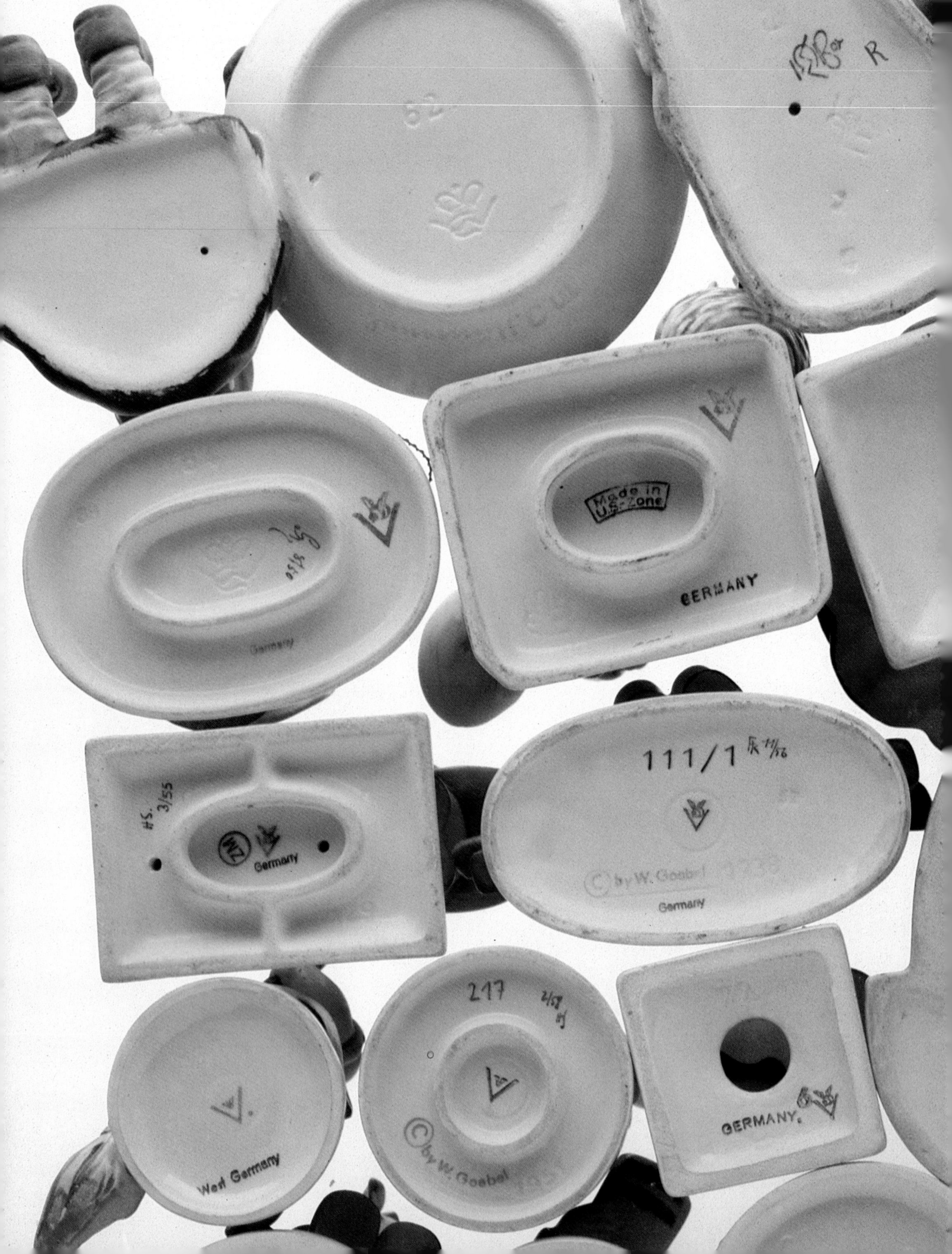

APPENDIX: A HISTORY OF THE MARKS AND SYMBOLS

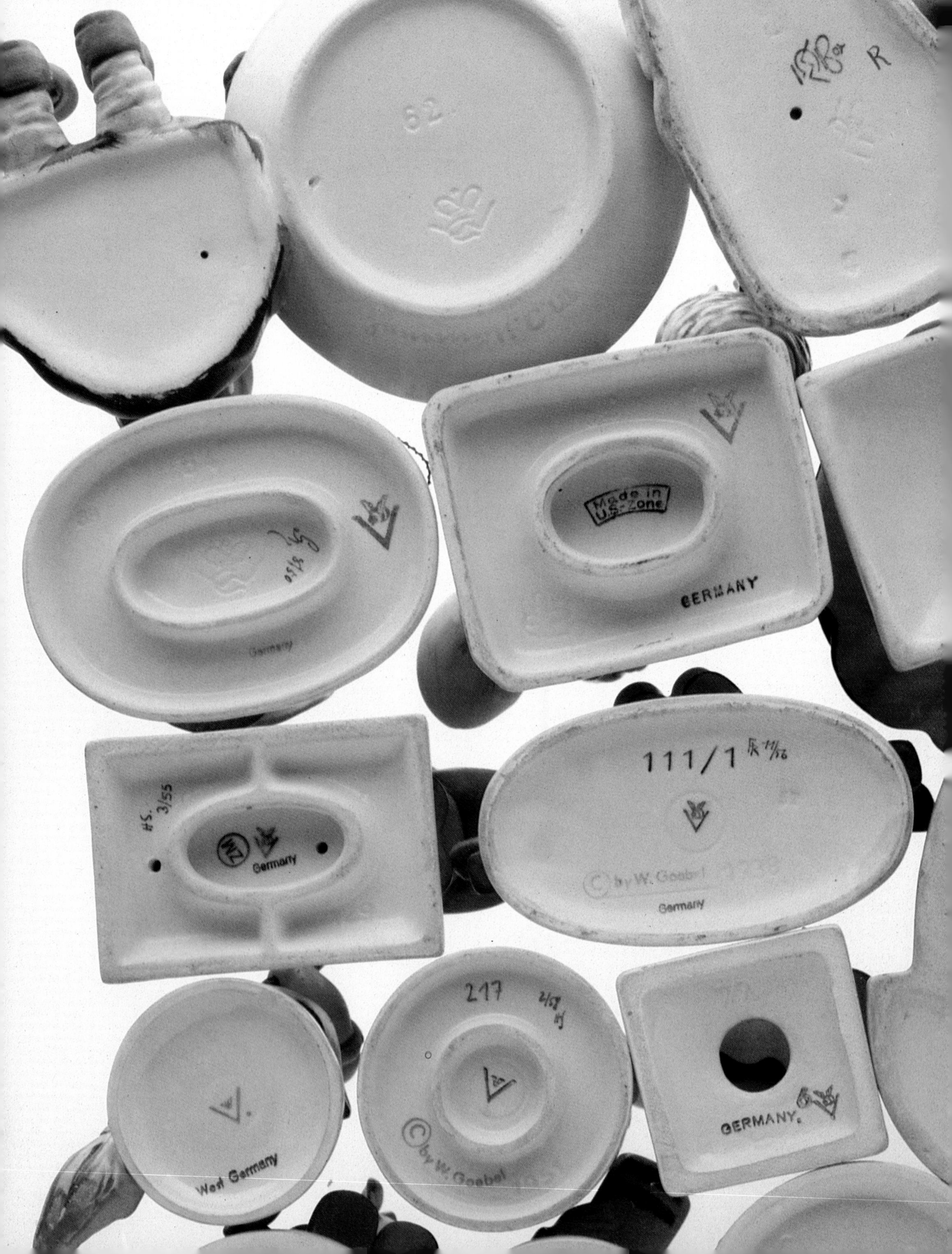

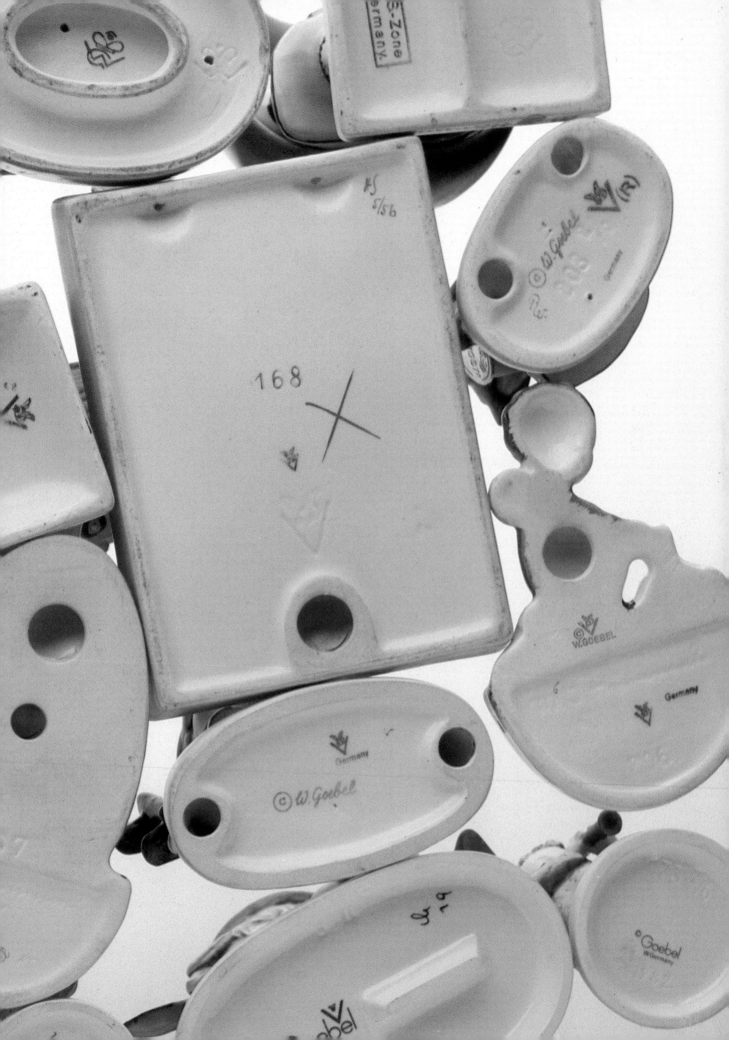

A History of Marks and Symbols

In celebration of the reunification of Germany, Goebel created a new backstamp for M. I. Hummel ceramics only. Effective January 1, 1991, it incorporates a "wide-crown WG" mark with the company name, and "Germany" as the country of origin.

While this new backstamp does not constitute a new trademark for Goebel, its significance is not lost on collectors. Over the years, any change in the backstamp has been a source of excitement, for it makes "new" that which has existed before. Following is a detailed history of the marks and symbols, compiled and written by Robert L. Miller, the well-known collector.

A number of different marks have been used since 1935. The "wide-crown WG" trademark was used on the first figurines produced in 1935. On the earliest ones this mark was incised on the bottom of the base along with the "M. I. Hummel" signature on the top or side of the base. Between 1935 and 1955, the company occasionally used a ⊚ ⌇ mark on the side or top of the base of some models. This mark is sometimes seen to the right of the "M. I. Hummel" signature. The "crown" appears either incised or stamped. When both are used on the same piece, the mark is known as a "double crown." From 1946 through 1948, it was necessary to add the stamped words: "Made in the U.S. Zone Germany." This mark was used with various types of frames, or without a frame, underglazed or stamped over the glaze in black ink.

In 1950, four years after Sister Maria Innocentia Hummel's death, the company radically changed the trademark, as a tribute to her. The new trademark was a bee flying high in a "V." (*Hummel* means bumblebee in German, and the "V" stands for *Verkaufsgesellschaft*, or distribution company.) The mark, known as the "full bee" trademark, was used until 1955 and appeared—sometimes both incised and underglazed—in black or blue, and occasionally in green or magenta. In addition, the stamp "Germany," and later "West Germany," or "Western Germany," appeared. An (R) appearing beside the trademark stands for "registered" and has no other significance.

Sometimes the molds were produced with a lightly incised circle on the bottom of the base in which the trademark was centered. The circle has no significance other than as a target for the location of the decal.

The company continued to modify the trademark through the 1950s; in 1956, they made the bee smaller, with its wing tips parallel with the top of the "V" (it was still inside the "V"). In 1957, the bee rose slightly above the "V." In 1958, the bee became even smaller and it flew deep within the "V." The year 1959 saw the beginning of stylization and the wings of the bee became sharply angular.

In 1960, the completely stylized bee with "V" mark came into use, appearing with "W. Germany." This mark was used, in one form or another, until 1979. In addition to its appearance with "W. Germany" to the right of the mark (1960–1963), it appeared centered above the "W. Germany" (1960–1972), and to the left of the "three-line mark" (mid-1960s to 1972). The three-line mark was used intermittently, and sometimes concurrently, with the small stylized 1960–72 mark. It was the most prominent trademark in use prior to the "Goebel bee."

It eventually became apparent that the public was equating the "V and Bee" mark only with M. I. Hummel items and did not realize that it included the full scope of Goebel products. In 1972 the company introduced a printed "Goebel" with the stylized bee poised between the letters "b" and "e."

In 1979, the stylized bee was dropped. Only the name Goebel appeared. That same year, for the first time, the year of production was hand-lettered on the base next to the initials of the decorator who paints the face. And since 1991, the M. I. Hummel collectibles also bear the new "wide-crown WG," as described above.

Note: Most of the known marks used over the years are shown on the opposite page. However, from time to time, a rare and undocumented variation may surface.

1935–1949

1935–1955

M.J.Hümmel © ⟨bee mark⟩

Incised Crown   Stamped Crown

1946–1948

1950–1955

Incised   Stamped   Stamped (R)   Full Bee   Full Bee

1956   **1957**   **1958**   **1959**   **1957–1960**

Small Bee   High Bee   Baby Bee   V Bee   Early Stylized (Incised Circle)

1935–1955

Germany
West Germany
Western Germany
GERMANY

Western Germany

© W. Goebel

Copr. W. Goebel

1960–1963   **1960–1972**   **1964–1972**   **1972–1979**   **1979–1990**   **1991–**

W. Germany   W. Germany   © by W. Goebel W. Germany   Goebel W. Germany   Goebel ʀ W. Germany   Goebel Germany

305

Index

This index to chapters two and four is organized by category. It is an alphabetical listing, with the exception of dated series, which are listed in consecutive order. All the M. I. Hummel collectibles shown in this book are listed, as well as the special Little Bavaria series, although it is not produced by Goebel. The Collector's Log column is for any personal notes you may wish to make, such as date and place of acquisition.

Name	HUM Number	Page(s)	Collector's Log
Good Shepherd	42	36	
Goose Girl	47	95	
Grandma's Girl	561	44	
Grandpa's Boy	562	44	
Guiding Angel	357	155	
Happiness	86	137	
Happy Birthday	176	116	
Happy Days	150	142	
Happy Pastime	69	80, 130	
Happy Traveller	109	59	
Harmony in Four Parts	471	33	
Hear Ye! Hear Ye!	15	72	
Heavenly Angel	21	156	
Heavenly Lullaby	262	152	
Heavenly Protection	88	53	
Hello	124	120	
Hello World	429	168	
Helping Mother	325	150	
Holy Child	70	53	
Home from Market	198	66	
Homeward Bound	334	not shown	
Honey Lover	312	76, 83, 269	
Horse Trainer	423	129	
Hosanna	480	48	
I Brought You a Gift	479	76, 267	
I Forgot	362	126	
I Wonder	486	76, 88	
I Won't Hurt You	428	80	
I'll Protect Him	483	56	
I'm Here	478	51	
In D Major	430	132	
In the Meadow	459	47	
In the Orchard	461	41, 51	
In Tune	414	101	
Is It Raining?	420	109	
It's Cold	421	79	
Joyful	53	136	
Joyous News	27	156	
Jubilee	416	26, 49	
Just Dozing	451	56	
Just Fishing	373	95	
Just Resting	112	94, 95	

Name	HUM Number	Page(s)	Collector's Log
Mother's Helper	133	105	
Mountaineer	315	67	
My Wish Is Small	463	57	
Not For You!	317	90	
Off to School	329	66	
On Holiday	350	35, 114	
On Our Way	472	35	
On Secret Path	386	168	
One For You, One For Me	482	46	
One Hand, One Treat	493	77	
Out of Danger	56B	86	
Pay Attention	426	168	
Photographer	178	194, 196, 281	
Playmates	58	95	
Pleasant Journey	406	32, 70	
Pleasant Moment	425	124	
Postman	119	39	
Prayer Before Battle	20	129	
Puppy Love	1	139	
Relaxation	316	127	
Retreat to Safety	201	94	
Ride into Christmas	396	148	
Ring Around the Rosie	348	141	
Run-a-way, The	327	67, 68	
Sad Song	404	133	
Saint George	55	167	
Scamp	553	40	
School Boy	82	66, 108	
School Boys	170	102	
School Girl	81	108	
School Girls	177	103	
Sensitive Hunter	6	94, 279	
Serenade	85	135, 187	
She Loves Me, She Loves Me Not!	174	93	
Shepherd Boy	395	50	
Shepherd's Boy	64	95	
Shining Light	358	155	
Signs of Spring	203	193	
Sing Along	433	124	
Sing with Me	405	100	
Singing Lesson	63	91, 92	
Sister	98	96, 114	

Name	HUM Number	Page(s)	Collector's Log
True Friendship	402	82, 252	
Trumpet Boy	97	85	
Tuneful Angel	359	154	
Two Hands, One Treat	493	267	
Umbrella Boy	152A	61	
Umbrella Girl	152B	60	
Valentine Gift	387	78	
Valentine Joy	399	78	
Village Boy	51	169	
Visiting an Invalid	382	71	
Volunteers	50	64	
Waiter	154	120	
Wash Day	321	115, 187	
Watchful Angel	194	152	
Wayside Devotion	28	not shown	
Wayside Harmony	111	66	
Weary Wanderer	204	118	
We Congratulate	220, 214E, 260F	35, 65, 161, 163	
We Wish You the Best	600	33	
Well Done!	400	89, 158	
What Now?	422	78	
What's New?	418	104	
Where Are You?	427	168	
Where Did You Get That?	417	88	
Where Shall I Go?	465	46	
Which Hand?	258	65	
Whistlers' Duet	413	89	
Whitsuntide	163	155	
Will It Sting?	450	42	
Winter Song	476	48	
With Loving Greetings	309	150, 278	
Worship	84	169	
Young Scholar	464	40	

BELLS

Annual Series

Name	HUM Number	Page(s)	Collector's Log
1978 - Let's Sing	700	181	
1979 - Farewell	701	181	
1980 - Thoughtful	702	181	
1981 - In Tune	703	181	
1982 - She Loves Me	704	181	
1983 - Knit One	705	181	
1984 - Mountaineer	706	181	

Name	HUM Number	Page(s)	Collector's Log
1985 - Girl with Sheet of Music	707	181	
1986 - Sing Along	708	181	
1987 - With Loving Greetings	709	181	
1988 - Busy Student	710	181	
1989 - Latest News	711	181	
1990 - What's New?	712	181	
1991 - Favorite Pet	713	181	
1992 - Whistlers' Duet	714	181	

Christmas Series

Name	HUM Number	Page(s)	Collector's Log
1989 - Ride into Christmas	775	184	
1990 - Letter to Santa Claus	776	184	
1991 - Hear Ye! Hear Ye!	777	184	
1992 - Harmony in Four Parts	778	184	

PLATES

Annual Series

Name	HUM Number	Page(s)	Collector's Log
1971 - Heavenly Angel	264	25, 182	
1972 - Hear Ye! Hear Ye!	265	182	
1973 - Globe Trotter	266	182	
1974 - Goose Girl	267	182	
1975 - Ride into Christmas	268	182	
1976 - Apple Tree Girl	269	183	
1977 - Apple Tree Boy	270	182	
1978 - Happy Pastime	271	183	
1979 - Singing Lesson	272	183	
1980 - School Girl	273	183	
1981 - Umbrella Boy	274	183	
1982 - Umbrella Girl	275	183	
1983 - Postman	276	182	
1984 - Little Helper	277	182	
1985 - Chick Girl	278	182	
1986 - Playmates	279	182	
1987 - Feeding Time	283	182	
1988 - Little Goat Herder	284	183	
1989 - Farm Boy	285	182	
1990 - Shepherd's Boy	286	183	
1991 - Just Resting	287	183	
1992 - Wayside Harmony	288	183	
1993 - Doll Bath	289	184	
1994 - Doctor	290	184	
1995 - Come Back Soon	291	184	

Name	HUM Number	Page(s)	Collector's Log
Umbrella Boy	518	190	
Umbrella Girl	512	190	

HOLY WATER FONTS

Name	HUM Number	Page(s)	Collector's Log
Angel Cloud	206	170	
Angel Duet	146	170	
Angel facing left	91A	170	
Angel facing right	91B	170	
Angel Shrine	147	170	
Angel Sitting	167	170	
Angel with Bird	354C	173	
Angel with Birds	22	170	
Angel with Lantern	354A	173	
Angel with Trumpet	354B	173	
Child Jesus	26	170	
Child with Flowers	36	170	
Dove	393	170	
Good Shepherd	35	170	
Guardian Angel	29, 248	170, 173	
Heavenly Angel	207	170	
Holy Cross	77	170	
Holy Family	246	170	
Joyous News with Lute	241	173	
Joyous News with Trumpet	242	173	
Madonna and Child	243	170	
White Angel	75	170	
Worship	164	170	

KITCHEN MOLDS

Name	HUM Number	Page(s)	Collector's Log
A Fair Measure	670	185	
Baker	674	185	
Baking Day	669	185	
For Father	672	185	
Supper's Coming	673	185	
Sweet As Can Be	671	185	

TABLE LAMPS

Name	HUM Number	Page(s)	Collector's Log
Apple Tree Boy	230	147	
Apple Tree Girl	229	144	
Birthday Serenade	231, 234	144	
Culprits	44A	144	
Good Friends	228	147	
Happy Days	232, 235	144	

Name	HUM Number	Page(s)	Collector's Log
Just Resting	II/112, 225	147	
Out of Danger	44B	147	
She Loves Me, She Loves Me Not!	227	144	
To Market	101, 223	145	
Wayside Harmony	II/111, 224	147	

NATIVITY SETS AND COMPONENTS

Name	HUM Number	Page(s)	Collector's Log
Large set with wooden stable	260	162–163	
Angel Serenade	260E	153, 163	
Donkey	260L	162	
Good Night	260D	162	
Infant Jesus	260C	163	
King, kneeling	260P	not shown	
King, standing	260O	163	
Little Tooter	260K	162	
Madonna	260A	163	
Moorish King	260N	163	
Ox	260M	162	
Sheep, lying	260R	162	
Saint Joseph	260B	163	
Sheep, with lamb	260H	162	
Shepherd Boy	260J	162	
Shepherd	260G	162	
Set with wooden stable	214	160–161	
Angel Serenade	214D	160, 163	
Good Night	214C	161	
Donkey	214J	160	
Infant Jesus	214A	161	
Saint Joseph	214B	160	
King, on one knee	214M	161	
King, on two knees	214N	161	
Lamb	214O	152, 160	
Madonna	214A	161	
Moorish King	214L	161	
Ox	214K	160	
Shepherd, kneeling	214G	160	
Little Tooter	214H	160	
Shepherd, standing	214F	160	

ORNAMENT SERIES - DATED

Name	HUM Number	Page(s)	Collector's Log
1988 - Flying High	452	175	
1989 - Love from Above	481	175	
1990 - Peace on Earth	484	175	

Name	HUM Number	Page(s)	Collector's Log
1991 - Angelic Guide	571	175	
1992 - Light Up the Night	622	175	

ORNAMENT SERIES - UNDATED

Name	HUM Number	Page(s)	Collector's Log
Heavenly Angel	575	176	
Festival Harmony (Mandolin)	576	176	
Festival Harmony (Flute)	577	176	
Celestial Musician	578	176	
Song of Praise	579	176	
Angel with Lute	580	176	
Praying Angel	581	176	
Angel with Flute	582	176	
Angel in Cloud	585	176	
Angel with Trumpet	586	176	

PLAQUES

Name	HUM Number	Page(s)	Collector's Log
Ba-bee Ring	30A&B	178	
Being Punished	326	83	
Child in Bed	137	178	
Flitting Butterfly	139	178	
Little Fiddler	93	180	
Madonna and Child (in relief)	249	276	
Madonna	48	171	
Madonna (metal frame)	222	276	
Merry Christmas	323	174	
Merry Wanderer	92	180	
Quartet	134	180	
Retreat to Safety	126	180	
Searching Angel	310	174	
Smiling Through	690		
Standing Boy	168	180	
Swaying Lullaby	165	179	
The Mail is Here	140	180	
Tuneful Goodnight	180	172	
Vacation Time	125	180	

STORE DISPLAY PLAQUES

Name	HUM Number	Page(s)	Collector's Log
Merry Wanderer			
English	187A	276	
German	205	276	
The Tally	460	276	

WALL VASES

Name	HUM Number	Page(s)	Collector's Log
Boy/Girl	360A	185	

Name	HUM Number	Page(s)	Collector's Log
Boy	360B	185	
Girl	360C	185	

FIGURINE MINIATURES	Studio Design Marks		
Accordian Boy	266-P	187	
Apple Tree Boy	257-P	187	
Baker	262-P	187	
Busy Student	268-P	187	
Cinderella	264-P	187	
Doll Bath	252-P	187	
Little Fiddler	250-P	187	
Little Sweeper	253-P	187	
Merry Wanderer	254-P	187	
Merry Wanderer Display Plaque	280-P	187	
Postman	255-P	187	
Serenade	265-P	187	
Stormy Weather	251-P	187	
Visiting an Invalid	256-P	187	
Waiter	263-P	187	
We Congratulate	267-P	187	

FOUR SEASONS MUSIC BOXES	No HUM Number		
1987 - Ride into Christmas		177	
1988 - Chick Girl		177	
1989 - In Tune		177	
1990 - Umbrella Girl		177	
Christmas Plate Series			
1987 - Celestial Musician		176	
1988 - Angel Duet		176	
1989 - Christmas Song		176	
1990 - Tender Watch		176	

LITTLE BAVARIA SERIES			
Birthplace-Massing		285	
Grammar School		286	
Cathedral-Massing		288	
Institute of English Sisters at Simbach		286	
Munich Academy of Applied Arts		286	
Church at Convent of Siessen		not shown	